Basketry
The Shaker Tradition

Utility basket
probably of Maine Shaker origin

North Family portrait, Mt. Lebanon, N.Y.

Basketry
The Shaker Tradition

History • Techniques • Projects

John McGuire

Photography by Henry Peach

LARK BOOKS
A Division of Sterling Publishing Co., Inc.
New York

Church Family Kitchen shows a variety of kitchen objects and utilitarian baskets. Deep set windows and long Shaker work table with red wash base are particularly handsome.

Editor: Kate Mathews
Design: Thom Boswell and Rob Pulleyn
Cover Designer: Barbara Zaretsky

Library of Congress has cataloged the hardcover edition as follows:

McGuire, John E.
    Basketry: the Shaker tradition: history, techniques, projects.
    Includes index.
    ISBN 0-937274-46-1
    1. Basket making. 2. Art, Shaker. I. Title.
    TT879.B3M389 1988
    746.41'287-83653

10 9 8 7 6 5 4 3 2 1

Published by Lark Books, a division of
Sterling Publishing Co., Inc.
387 Park Avenue South, New York, N.Y. 10016

First Paperback Edition 2004
© 1989, John McGuire

Distributed in Canada by Sterling Publishing,
c/o Canadian Manda Group, One Atlantic Ave., Suite 105
Toronto, Ontario, Canada M6K 3E7

Distributed in the U.K. by Guild of Master Craftsman Publications Ltd.
Castle Place, 166 High Street, Lewes, East Sussex, England BN7 1XU
Tel: (+ 44) 1273 477374, Fax: (+ 44) 1273 478606
Email: pubs@thegmcgroup.com, Web: www.gmcpublications.com

Distributed in Australia by Capricorn Link (Australia) Pty Ltd.
P.O. Box 704, Windsor, NSW 2756 Australia

If you have questions or comments about this book, please contact:
Lark Books
67 Broadway
Asheville, NC 28801
(828) 253-0467

Manufactured in China

ISBN 0-937274-46-1 (hardcover) 1-57990-606-0 (paperback)

Dedication.

To the Rev. Chester D. Freeman, Jr. whose tireless efforts made this book a reality, and to the Shakers who provided the inspiration.

Stereoscopic view of a Shaker school

Acknowledgements.

My appreciation and thanks are extended to Barbara and Charles Adams for sharing their collection and to Cheryl Anderson whose knowledge as the first Director of Education at Hancock was of great benefit. Sincere appreciation is extended to my Hancock "family," both staff and directors past and present. I owe a debt of gratitude to Christine M. Gregg Ph.D. for her help and clarity. Thanks to Joan Huntington, whose collection gives breadth to the antique section, and to Brian Lewis for sharing his photographs of Hancock's buildings and grounds. Sincere gratitude is due Robert Meader whose preface adds much to this volume; his quiet dedication to the Shakers as former director of the Shaker Museum at Old Chatham, New York, and as Hancock's librarian/archivist cannot be overlooked. Continuing thanks to Henry E. Peach; his photographic genius and friendship enriches each book we do together. (Miscellaneous photo credits appear on page 144.) Thanks to Bill Senseney and his family for sharing their home and making my seasons at Hancock possible and enjoyable. Finally, my appreciation to Andrew Vadnais, director of Mount Lebanon Shaker Village Museum, and Darrow School History Department for their assistance. A special note of appreciation to those involved with the production of this book: Kate Mathews, Thom Boswell and Rob Pulleyn.

Contents.

Shaker utility basket
hosts a variety of hand-dyed yarns.
Note the strong and well-formed handles
at the ends of the basket.

Preface.

John E. McGuire's new book superbly illustrates his
fascination with the Shakers and his discovery of their community basketmaking industry.
This book also includes an informative chapter on baskets which are often mistaken for
Shaker, such as the "bushwhacker" or Taghkanic baskets of Columbia County, New York,
as well as Native American and German baskets.

A master basketmaker and lecturer on the subject, McGuire's interest in Shaker work
was sparked approximately twenty years ago and has culminated in this book and his
serving as a demonstrating interpreter at Hancock Shaker Village in Pittsfield, Massachusetts. He is concerned not only with the technical artistry of Shaker basketry and the
infinite variety of forms, but equally with the dedicated makers themselves — as people and
as members of a celibate religious order. Sister R. Mildred Barker of the Sabbathday Lake,
Maine Shakers recently remarked a bit wistfully that she hoped to be remembered as a
person and not as a chair! This is what John E. McGuire has done —presented the Shakers
as talented and dedicated people.

Chair makers were said to bear in mind, while building a chair, that one day an angel
might sit upon it. Such a celestial messenger might also use a basket to collect apples, make

*Variety of Shaker and other types of storage baskets with barrels and buckets located in the Church Family
Dwelling basement*

cheese, or even to hunt for a needle and thread to mend a robe. Whatever the shape or size, all baskets were equally worthy. It's no wonder they have always been avidly sought by collectors and dealers.

In their day Shaker baskets were relatively inexpensive, even by the standards of the time. Baskets served the purposes of today's paper bags, cardboard cartons, and shopping bags, but they were vastly more durable. Even now, after decades of hard use, remarkably few are so dilapidated as to be disreputable or unusable. This is a tribute both to the materials employed and the methods of manufacture. Until late Victorian days when canons of simplicity and lack of ostentation where somewhat relaxed, the Believers avoided "superfluities" of color and decorative weaving. Mother Ann admonished her Shaker followers to do everything as if they had a thousand years to live *and* as they would do if they knew they would die on the morrow. This meticulous attention to detail, even when unnecessary, is what has made all Shaker work so cherished.

This, then, is John E. McGuire's objective — to make real and living the craftspeople and the work of their hands. For not only did they make superb baskets, they also raised and shingled magnificent buildings, built dams and mills, and labored in myriad ways to make their homes a little bit of heaven and to share that heavenly vision with others. Through the pages of this book the reader will get glimpses of the lives, the labors, and the dreams of the Believers in Christ's Second Appearing.

Robert F.W. Meader
Hancock Shaker Village
Pittsfield, Massachusetts
December, 1988

(Riddle) or sieve

Introduction.

If you are the least bit sensitive to what the Shakers are about, you are no doubt awed by their range of talents and their ability to put those talents to the best use — from Shakers as members of a separatist communal society stressing equality of the sexes to Shakers as craftspeople building for the millenium. I have found that those who know the least about the Shakers remember their society for the array of products they made. A reader of a book about the Shakers or a visitor to a Shaker community can't help but note the neat and ordered look of their buildings and lands or the supreme attention to detail. In the brick dwelling at Hancock Shaker Village, more than 4,000 hand-turned pegs set in rails outlining rooms and hallways entreated Believers to keep things neat. Chairs and multitudes of other items were hung from these pegs, giving precision to an already well-conceived space.

As a resident basketmaker for Hancock Shaker Village Museum, I came to understand and better appreciate this Society. Anecdotes and bits of information would surface during my conversations with interpreters and craftspeople. Periodic revelations came from visitors and scholars of the Shakers, some in the form of home photographs and one astounding newsreel of the Shakers at Mt. Lebanon at Christmas. These stories are retold here to help you feel and experience the Shakers, to convey why the Shakers came to be.

Too many people see the pictures of the stony-faced Brothers and Sisters and think what a chore it must have been to exist as a Shaker. Surely it wasn't without sacrifice, but people fail to remember that there were no bars on the windows — one could leave at will. Yet the faces frozen on tin and paper seem to deny the joy. Consider the photographic process of the 1800s — its novelty was a bit scary and models had to hold their positions for minutes at a time. As the years and technology progressed, the faces relax and the warmth comes through.

While the primary focus of this book is on Shaker basketry, it has turned out to be much more. It is impossible to separate basketry, out of context, from anything the Shakers made. It is also impossible to ignore what ignited the Shakers to produce such items. To that end I have shown buildings, interiors, and artifacts, but most of all I have tried to show the humanity and spirituality, for it is all part of the Shaker experience. I have portrayed those dedicated to basketry as a craft or profession and the precise way they constructed their work. Above all, I have attempted to show why these Believers would found their villages and become a part of history so unique that they will endure long after their passing.

Grace Bowers, Martha Anderson, Anna White

*Pharmacy display in
the Church Family Dwelling.*

*Oak swing handle basket: controversy exists con-
cerning the Shaker manufacture of such baskets.
While perhaps not sold, their manufacture seems
clear.*

The tradition.

Travel and travail.

It is hard to describe charisma but it is something that Ann Lee clearly possessed. This lady with a message and an unusual destiny was born in England in 1736 and was certainly a bit out of the ordinary. Little is known about this illiterate "prophetess" except that her marriage was a failure and her four children died very young.

Ann Lee was an Anglican turned Quaker, so her spirituality was probably very strong and her mission unique. She embraced a Quaker splinter group founded in 1747 by the Wardleys of Bolton, near Manchester, Lancashire. The group's uniqueness was evident in its seizures and trances, as well as its meekness, simplicity, and pacifism.

Her close circle of friends (soon to be followers) found in Ann something that must have struck a spiritual chord in their own lives. Far from the usual quiet practice of religion, this splinter group would choose a physical and vocal demonstration of their faith and the way they wished to worship God. Whatever was special about Ann was to permeate their lives, promote change, and launch them into a quest for free religious expression.

Some would argue that Ann was psychologically a prime candidate for celibacy, given her painful marriage. Yet it must have been more than her tragic losses that moved her to espouse the celibate lifestyle that would become one of the pillars on which this fledgling faith would stand. Those who followed her would find that in forsaking marriage, a greater bond with God and their fellow believers was possible. Ann's own marriage to an illiterate blacksmith was to fall victim to her spirituality. It was this struggle and subsequent Divine revelations that would convince the small group that Ann was indeed God's conduit on earth and that she should become their leader — Mother Ann.

The Shakers were so vocal and exuberant in the practice of their faith that they were frequently considered to be "a disruptive element" in society. Their religious demonstrations were the cause of their many brushes with the law. In fact, Ann's life often conflicted

Antique printing of the principles of Shaker faith

"The principal doctrines of the Shakers are,—a belief in the *second appearance of Christ*, in the person of the holy mother. They admit of but two persons in the Godhead, God the Father, and God the Mother, which they say is according to the order of nature, being male and female. To redeem the depraved race of man, they believe that it became necessary for God to take upon him the real character of human nature as it is, male and female, and that his first appearance was in the person of man, and the second in the person of woman, whereby the work of redemption was finished and completed. The confusion and wickedness that prevailed in the Catholic Church, during the long period which preceded and followed the reformation, they ascribe to the work of redemption not being completed in Christ's first appearance, it being the necessary period that must intervene between the making and fulfillment of the promise of Christ, that he would establish his law of righteousness on earth. They believe in perfect holiness, and insist that salvation from *sin* here is necessary to salvation from misery hereafter.

with those in power as she became her followers' spiritual authority. However, the frequent clashes with the law and with their neighbors did not diminish the Shakers' zeal. Rather, it served to strengthen their resolve.

God finally spoke to Mother Ann and revealed His plan for her to lead her followers to America in 1774. Wherever they went, many would find this small group of believers to be a problem. Consider the fact that, in a masculine world, a woman was believed to be the wellspring of God's will. It was most unusual for a woman to hold such power and authority; how unusual was to become even more evident as time passed. A near sinking of their ship and its "miraculous" repair only reassured the believers of God's might and convinced them that in Ann Lee and her teachings salvation was possible.

To Mother Ann a revelation of the duality of God as both masculine and feminine, distinct yet one, was revealed. Her teachings, which became the basis of the Shaker faith, frequently contradicted those of the more established churches. In fact, Ann was briefly imprisoned on a charge of blasphemy even before her arrival in America.

Mother Ann's next major revelation was that freedom from sin could only be found in the abandonment of self-indulgent sex. She preached that only through celibacy could God's higher purposes be better served. No doubt this was the final blow to her fragile marriage; her husband abandoned her shortly after his arrival on these shores.

The Shakers arrived in this country with little means and were met with growing suspicion. The small band, which included Ann's brother, dispersed to survive and prosper until conditions were more favorable. Nearly a year later they regrouped near Albany, New York and hastily built log cabins to prepare for an anticipated

Poem by Eldress Dorothy of Shaker Village, East Canterbury, N.H., admonishes Brother Tyler to do work in virtue and honor Mother Ann's ways.

Utility and storage baskets located in the laundry area of the Machine Shop at Hancock Shaker Village

growing flock. The growth so eagerly awaited simply was not to be and so this dedicated band began to clear lands and improve their structures, always in anticipation of new believers.

In 1779 a disillisioned group of New Light Baptists provided the thrust that the Shakers needed. In New Lebanon, New York, these millennialists awaited the second coming of Christ and were looking for a sinless way to live. In this setting Mother Ann and her followers found fruitful ground — these potential converts felt that the Shaker faith offered them a path to salvation.

The Shakers were buoyed with this wave of conversions in 1780. Through confession of sins, a vow of celibacy, and obedience to the Society, the ranks had grown to such proportions that in 1781 Mother Ann and a few followers set out to preach the Gospel and proselytize the faith in Massachusetts, Connecticut, New Hampshire, and what is now called Maine. As always, problems accompanied Ann's work, warrants were issued for her arrest, and physical beatings occurred. Mother Ann's "calling" and the Biblical scriptures regarding suffering must have been the inspiration to keep her going. As the number of believers increased, the early Shaker Church had its own disruptive elements. Sometimes important converts became critics when advancement in the church hierarchy was not rapid enough to suit them.

It was the frequency of problems, arduous travel, and frequent beatings that caused others to take over Mother Ann's work. In 1783 Ann died at the age of 48, after seeing only

Antique woodcut showing the Shakers dancing as part of their religious expression. Note the separation of the sexes.

North Family portrait, Mt. Lebanon, N.Y.

Street at Church Family, Mt. Lebanon, N.Y.

a small portion of her dream accomplished. However, she had firmly instilled her vision in others and laid the foundation for a Society of 18 communities and more than 6,000 believers. It wasn't until later, when Mother Ann's body was examined and reburied, that a fracture in her skull that perhaps caused her death was discovered. The grieving believers who suffered Ann's loss certainly found comfort in the image of her Christ counterpart. The Church would only blossom after her or His death, an after effect not without historical precedent in other churches.

Ann's work was left in the hands of a few followers who consecrated their lands and possessions to their religion. The Goodrich, Talcott, and Deming families figured prominently in this formative period. During this time spiritual authority was transferred from the original settlement at Watervliet (Niskayuna) in New York to the now developing community at New Lebanon. This settlement was formed by Ann's hand-picked successor, Father James Whittaker, an English disciple who had followed her to America. He was the prime force behind attracting a group of converts that will endure into the 21st century. New Lebanon was the spiritual center of authority for the Shaker faith and the nucleus for future expansion into other areas.

In 1787 Elder Joseph Meacham succeeded Whittaker as the first American-born leader. His leadership enjoyed the benefits of his predecessor's faculty for gathering converts and centralizing memberships that were once scattered. Under Meacham's guidance the communal living at New Lebanon was "ordered" and Shaker doctrine and organization was formalized. In 1795 Meacham created a formal covenant that replaced the rather unspecific verbal covenant. Records have revealed that although the "community of goods" was practiced and individual donations were recorded upon entry, no such specific covenant had existed.

In 1790 the growing interest and membership in the Hancock area attracted Meacham's attention and he sent an Elder to bring the believers at Hancock into Gospel order. Calvin Harlow became Hancock's first Bishop and spiritual leader of the believers in Enfield, Connecticut. It wasn't a surprise for many when he assumed such prominence because Mother Ann had prophesied "great glories" for this believer as early as 1783. To complete the leadership of the new settlement, Sarah Harrison was appointed Eldress, and gathering into the church of Hancock began in 1791.

Cecelia DeVere (Mt. Lebanon, N.Y.)

Stereoscopic view of Canterbury, N.H. brothers

Mt. Lebanon Meeting House circa 1930

The early Church, formally called The United Society of Believers in Christ's Second Appearing, was not without a period of confusion and transition. Founding a fledgling church with new believers, given all the new requirements for membership, was difficult.

A basic tenet of the faith was the complete separation of the Shaker communities from the world and its goods. The original members had divested themselves of their worldly goods or else donated their lands and possessions to the Church. Others wished to join and work out the temporal affairs of their life later on. Still others wished to experience this community and faith as novices. The different classes of believers were ordered into "families" which were first named by those in authority, and later named according to their geographical location relative to the Church and to each other. For example, the West family was west of the church. It is important to remember that the designation of the word "family" was in the highest sense of the word; traditional family ties were no longer part of members' faith or vocabulary. Variations in the prescribed order of the Church allowed for

Restored Round Stone Barn at Hancock.

flexibility during this transitional period, which was necessary for the Church to grow.

As the communities grew, the naming of additional "families" varied. In the Hancock order, the Second (Middle, in other communities) family was used to designate a family located in between the established groups.

The first and foremost community or Mother House was that of New Lebanon, New York. In accordance with the basic tenet of equality of the sexes, the central Ministry consisted of two Elders and two Eldresses. The central Ministry resided at New Lebanon and was the final arbiter of spiritual and temporal matters.

The next level of authority was the Bishopric of Hancock, whose direction included that of Tyringham, Massachusetts, as well as Hancock and Enfield, Connecticut. Composed of two Elders and two Eldresses, the Bishopric was involved with spiritual and temporal direction of the communities under their authority.

Immediately under this chain of authority was the Church family. This primary family was comprised of the early converts or "Old Believers," who had achieved independence from the world and had been the driving force for the establishment of Hancock from its earliest moments until its final dissolution in 1959.

The Junior Order, consisting of the West and Second families, comprised those who still had entanglements with their finances or some other hindrance, but they enjoyed the benefits of a united inheritance. This order consisted of those people who had never been

Poultry House, Hancock Shaker Village

married, but until a final decision on membership was reached, retained control over their property and family ties.

The Novitiate or First Order consisted of the East and South families. Members by verbal agreement only, they were under scrutiny. After complete divestiture and joining of the covenant were they fully part of the faith. In 1790 a written covenant was adopted giving further solidification to the faith and formally outlining what were the responsibilities of all. The novitiate was admitted into full membership as the Third or Church order. Heading each of these families were two Elders and two Eldresses. These leaders were responsible for the spiritual health of the individual families, which were autonomous financial units, and were subordinate to the Church family.

Along with the spiritual needs, the temporal affairs of each family were directed by two Brethren and two Sisters who, as Trustees, handled the legal and financial affairs of the family as specified in the Millennial Laws. The term Trustees or office deacons or office sisters can be used interchangeably here. The internal economic affairs of running the shops, dwellings, kitchen, and farm remained in the control of the two Family Deacons and two Deaconesses and were divided along traditional lines. The Deacons made final decisions about the farms and some shops, and Deaconesses about the kitchens, dwellings, and other shops.

Ice House and Tan House

It must be noted that while equality of the sexes was a primary tenet of the faith, division of labor was not without thought to ability and tradition, along the lines of what would be considered "sexist" today. At no time was this thought to be anything but total equality.

Another area of responsibility involved the "children of converts" and "orphans" who were raised in the hopes of expanding the membership of faith as well as bringing more hands to labor. They were placed in the loving care of a Brother or Sister chosen for such talents.

It must be remembered that no person was born a Shaker and one of the major tenets of Shaker faith was a celibate lifestyle. The obvious way the Shakers expected to flourish was by conversion of members from the outside world. The use of "world's people" as a designation referring to people outside the faith and physically outside of the geographic boundaries of the community was to become the standard way of referring to non-believers. If conversion was the only way to faith, a young Church needed to be flexible and in some cases forgiving. This flexibility and the belief that revelation was ongoing allowed the Church to adapt to the needs of the believers and encouraged membership.

This sect required early believers to endure hardships and struggle. Accounts refer to as many as 14 men living in one room and some references to diet indicate that in the beginning the Shakers existed on precious little at times. The religious fervor of the time and a great sense of shared struggle enabled the people to endure. Joined by converts that were moneyed and successful or farmers and artisans, this humble and unconventional religion began to take root in New England.

It was believed that the Shakers were experiencing Heaven on earth and this existence required an organization that left little to the imagination. As the spiritual Heaven was thought to be tidy and beautiful, as well as without problems, so were all the Shaker communities organized and built to mirror this divine inspiration.

The Hancock community was blessed with the talents of joiners, masons, farmers, and the like. By 1820 the Hancock Church family buildings numbered 34; the buildings later

included an astonishing and expensive $10,000 round stone barn begun in 1825 and a massive brick dwelling built in 1830 to house nearly 100 members. These and other buildings of the Hancock community testify to the rise of the Shakers and their industry.

Beyond the physical changes to the community, spiritual and temporal changes were also taking place. Every aspect of communal life was controlled, from the color of the buildings to the placing of the right leg into a pair of trousers first. School was taught with regard for the workings of the community and its economic base, and the work ethic was instilled at a very early age. Even the youngest children were given tasks equal to their strength and abilities. Apprenticed children and adopted orphans comprised a good source of potential converts. They were lovingly raised and well educated.

Growth also was reflected in membership. The central Church family grew so large as to require the addition of a North family in 1821. The ebb and flow of believers is evident in early census records that indicate tens of thousands passing in and out of the communities.

The city of peace.

This self-given "spiritual name" reflects the nature and physical appearance of Hancock: well-cared for buildings, fields tended with the utmost respect, subtle and painterly colors, and everywhere a subdued mode of dress and manner. How beguiling it must have been for people seeking God in a young nation struggling to find its identity.

Certainly after the horrors of the War of Independence, the prospect of a millennium of peace, free from inequality, must have had great appeal. Women who had lost their husbands, either in war or through natural causes and who wished not to remarry, could find a ready haven. As Shakers, they were even freed from the responsibilities of rearing their own children — now brothers and sisters in faith. Men who tired of the daily struggle of providing for families could find in the Shaker faith an outlet for their creative efforts without the competition that caused some to grow rich while others remained caught in the spiral of struggle. The religion offered a communal sharing that created a security and peace without exacting one's last measure of effort.

Colorful variety of Shaker cloaks made for sale

I think that those who found it hard to believe that Mother Ann's was the Second Coming could still find enough other attractions to generate belief. I do not wish to belittle this fundamental principle of the Shakers, but as times changed, so too did the beliefs of those practicing the faith. Mother Ann's central importance was without question, but as the Shakers changed their thoughts about food, drink, and tobacco, they began to portray Mother Ann more as a prophet and continuing source of revelation after her death.

Early on, Hancock Village grew in numbers and achieved great success. However, after the 1860s there was a rapid decline in membership which was never reversed. Among the probable causes for the decline were the Industrial Revolution, the opening of the Western frontier, and a decrease in religious fervor. The first signs of membership decline are clear in records showing that women and children comprised the bulk of the Believers in the 1840s. This religion required new converts to survive and the attractions that interested people in joining slowly eroded as technology advanced.

How difficult it must have been to select leaders whose direction and advice would nurture a community and attract converts. On occasion the Leadership brought glimmers of hope and some recovery, but the gradual decline became accepted and was finally replaced with a serenity of resignation that the world was no longer ready for the Shakers.

Group photo of cloak makers

There was a millennial consideration in all that the

Shakers manufactured. It was believed that through Mother Ann, the second millennium had arrived and though she died, her teachings remained and believers continued to experience Christ. Therefore the millennium went on. If Heaven was to be on earth for a thousand years, then certainly the Shakers attempted to build items to last for that period of time. Nearly everything constructed for the outside "worldly" consumer reflected this dedication. Items made for their own use did not always reflect this extreme dedication, but the Shakers were always aware of their public image.

Another reason for the Shaker's dedication to the perfection of well-designed items was their lack of extraneous decoration. Ornamentation was considered a worldly affectation and Shakers believed manufacturing must be without such extras. An article made for sale can be carried along by elements extraneous to its basic design, to the point where the item's glitter conceals the lack of soundness. By stripping an article down to its most fundamental elements, little is left to the imagination — the piece either stands or falls on its own. Contemporary people refer to this idea as "form following function."

Still another contributing element to the beauty and simplicity of Shaker work was the lack of pressure to survive. Successful communal efforts meant sufficient time could be spent to reflect "heaven on earth" and all products therefore benefitted. I also believe the final contributing element to such manufacturing perfection was the issue of celibacy. Few modern thinkers will deny that when sublimated, sexual drive produces unexpected energies. When focused, this energy can have dramatic effects on creativity or productivity. Couple this with religious fervor and you have a tremendous force for the perfection of work.

The Shaker belief in Heaven on earth was fundamental. Frequent references to the need for perfection are found in their writings, as well as exhortations to create items heavenly enough to be worthy of a visiting angel. When you combine religion with such a philosophy, it is not hard to believe that such spiritual people could have viewed their work as a tangible prayer.

The Shakers made multitudes of items that were sought after by the buying public. These ranged from the most recognizable oval box with its "swallowtail" fingers to Shaker cloaks. So popular were these items that even the White House was a customer — Grover Cleveland's wife attended his second inauguration wearing a Shaker cloak. A legend is told that the first one made was a reject; it seems that the Shakers found it flawed and replaced it with a second prior to shipment.

This ready commerce with the public enabled the Shakers to feel the pulse of the buying world, and they industriously worked to meet those consumer needs. A quick survey of the buildings built and used by the Church family testifies to the Shakers' progressive activities. These included: a garden house, poultry house, dwelling house, brethren's shop, sister's shop, Ministry house, round stone barn, dairy wing, tannery, ice house, Deacon's shop, garden seed shop, hired men's quarters, cattle barn, Trustees office, office privy, wagon and grain sheds, cemetery, school house, horse barn, Ministry shop, meeting house, wood house, machine shop and

Dining table and chairs, Church Family Dwelling

laundry, hatter's shop, laundry wood house, corn drying house, nurse shop, ash house, summer house, brethren's privy, poultry incubator, dairy work house, sister's privy, boy's shop, broom shop and warehouse, milk house, slaughter house, corn crib, tin shop, tool house, office barn, carriage shed, blacksmith shop, boy's privy, girl's privy, school house wood shed, horse stand, lumber shed, garden tool shed, and foundations of other buildings whose functions are unknown.

Obviously this sect that preached separation from the world and its wicked ways was not out of touch. In fact, the Shakers frequently adapted ideas from the outside world that would make their industries more efficient and their lives more complete. After all, the Shakers gave up a large part of their individual autonomy and fused it into one Family. As the worldly way of life became more attractive, the Shakers had to create an atmosphere that would attract and hold converts because they needed every possible believer to continue their Faith.

The list of Shaker-built items was almost endless and their individual and collective efforts produced some contemporary conveniences that we take for granted. The washing machine and the flat broom are but two of their many contributions. Several attributions, including the round or circular saw blade, are flattering but incorrect. The Shakers eagerly adopted many innovations, leading to the mistaken belief that they were also the inventors.

The Shakers were also great salespeople. After all, they had great quality, simple yet elegant products, and a cost factor that at first enabled them to be very competitive. It's no wonder that the buying public beat a path to their door. The Trustees even sold Shaker

North Family sister weaving poplar/palm into cloth

wares in traveling exhibits set up in the lobbies of fine hotels; here their wares could be shown to a more monied clientele. It was not unusual to see journal entries attesting to the productivity of the community and individual families that vied for the marketplace. Tens of thousands of items including baskets were made and sold to the public. In addition to the Shaker traveling exhibits and individual sales at the Trustees office, there was a large network of retailers who were regular buyers. Included on this list is the famed Marshall Field store that sold Shaker wares in Chicago.

It was the perfectly constructed furniture that spoke so eloquently for the Shakers. Its beauty of line, understated elegance, and enduring quality all became hallmarks of this separate society.

If the Shakers chose to produce an item, they did so without cutting corners regardless of the cost. Frequently they held on to industries outsiders considered outdated. It has always been my theory that converts are attracted to a new faith because of the "little things" as well as the more obvious. What more attractive silent preacher for the Shaker faith could there be than the items produced by these people of peace?

What happened? The supply of potential converts began to dry up. Mismanagement, spiritual renewals that didn't fit the times or the psyches of the Believers, and lack of dynamic leadership brought decline. Most dramatically, the seemingly plush yet simple surroundings of the Shakers, which were once the envy of many in the outside world, came within the grasp of nearly all. Industrialization gave rise to a growing middle class. Men no longer joined, the children grew up and left the community, leaving aging women to "man" the shops and sell the wares. These factors were most evident after the Civil War. Although the Shakers were successful in bargaining a conscientious objector status and thus did not lose men to the war, they lost them to the world.

This sect, not unfamiliar with struggle, began to look to the world to provide male help. Married men were hired and they commuted to work. Unmarried men were housed in hired hands' quarters and in later years, married hired men and their families were also housed in Shaker buildings. Tobacco, once thought a gift and used by the Shakers, was now enjoyed only by the hirelings.

The Shakers never wavered on the fundamentals, though. Women were never allowed to visit the hired hands' quarters.

A Shaker brother from Watervliet, New York is credited as producing the first flat brooms.

Separation of the sexes applied to family members who visited converts and stayed in the Trustees' living quarters; they were never allowed joint room occupancy with their spouses or families.

Visitors to the Shaker Museum at Hancock frequently propose that if the Shakers had only adapted, they would have endured. I am sure that this refers to the celibacy issue. I believe this statement reflects the misconception that lack of families was the cause for decline when, in fact, this was only a minor aspect. As far as adaptation is concerned, the Shakers did indeed adapt and adopt things that would make it attractive to join. As late as the Victorian era, architecture was updated in a futile effort to show the world that the Shakers were still in touch, aware, and modern. The lace curtains that hung in the windows of the Trustees' house attested to a relaxed environment, but membership had so declined that the hoped for recovery was never to happen.

Herb Drying Area with grouping of different Shaker baskets

I was not there when the remaining Sisters left Han-cock after it was sold in 1959. It must have been a most bittersweet day. Certainly the Sisters had hope that their village would return to some of its understated splendor. Yet to leave a home, to leave memories, to leave departed Brothers and Sisters buried at Hancock must have been very difficult. I do not wish to imply that the survivors were caught up in materialism; their selling price for the village demonstrates the opposite. Yet no one leaves memories without a look back or a tear, even when one's whole purpose was to prepare to enter a more Heavenly Kingdom in the next world. The simple marker that stands like a

Corner grouping of Indian baskets shows the Shakers close relationship with Native Americans

sentinel in the cemetery at Hancock says it best: "In loving memory of members of the Shaker Church who dedicated their lives to God and to the good of humanity passed to immortality."

It must have been a great comfort to the Sisters that the dedicated people who bought these sacred lands were familiar faces, friends they had come to know. The buyers, now the Trustees of the Hancock Shaker Village Museum, had been some of the sensitive collectors of both artifacts and history. Now they are the inheritors of history. Many of these people felt that preservation of the deteriorating buildings would require all their efforts and vast sums of capital. Yet to turn Hancock into a thriving commercial venture, which would be necessary to generate such capital, must have seemed potentially profane. The magnificent round stone barn was in near ruins. The massive brick dwelling had been abandoned by the few remaining Shakers in favor of the Trustee's house and the vast number of buildings belonging to the thriving independent families of Hancock had been reduced.

Hancock has since grown into a historic landmark visited by thousands of curious yet respectful people. As staff was added to these restored architectural gems, a more complete image of the Shakers and their faith began to emerge. This process evolved with the help of the Sisters who watched over the growth of the museum and contributed to the historical accuracy of the interpretive staff. No living Shakers reside at Hancock and yet few visitors fail to feel the Shaker presence as they tour the land and visit their spaces.

Swallow tail oval box for a bonnet, yellow washed color. Probable work of master boxmaker Elder Daniel Crosman of New Lebanon (1810 - 1885).

No stage of my career as a historical basketmaker

brings back more intense feelings than the season at Hancock, when I was hired to create a basketmaking exhibit. My simple room was without a stove, but it did have electricity. The room also had two windows now showing the ravages of age and years of neglect. Fresh paint masked the lack of what would have been attentive care if only the brethren were there.

The Shakers enjoyed and installed modern and convenient labor-saving devices throughout their history — one only needs to visit the brick dwelling and see how running water fed from their reservoir brought water into their large steam kettles. To work at one's labor was a work of prayer, but to labor when more efficient methods were available seemed contrary to the Shakers.

My shop was above a converted tannery that had been abandoned and put to better, more diversified use. The basement floor still housed the buried tanning vats, but the area now demonstrates cider pressing. The second floor houses a woodworking area, although this was probably not where the Shakers did most of their work, for their machine shop was a marvel of water-powered equipment. This was where the hired hands probably did woodworking. The blacksmith shop that shared the basement once housed a triphammer that pounded the ash for Shaker baskets. One only needs to pound ash by hand to know the wisdom of using this machine.

This area was to be my "home" in every sense of the word. Throughout that summer I began to understand the Shakers' choice of Hancock for their village. Iron ore, which the Shakers smelted, was found in the surrounding hills and from my window I would see the night sky dance in a spectacular display as lightning hit those deposits.

I couldn't help but reflect on the serenity of the setting and yet its obvious commercial potential, being located near transportation routes, was not overlooked. The intrusive sounds of noisy tractor trailers on the highway frequently reminded me that "commerce" as well as "faith" was what the Shakers were about.

My work area was filled with old machines, planes, and workbenches so clearly the work of meticulous craftsmen. In time, a subtle yet distinct change took place in my work habits and craftsmanship. This "City of Peace" was aptly named — except for an occasional bleat of a newborn lamb, my early mornings were without interruption. My work pace slowed and the quality improved by the end of that first summer. It was as if the work ethic of the Shakers had become my own.

All staff members are paid to interpret Shaker work through their own work. In fact, craftspeople frequently disregard personal profit to re-create outstanding products of Shaker artistry. Interest in the Shakers from worldwide visitors and film crews, who attempt to capture the unique beauty of Shaker craftsmanship with their cameras, never seems to lag. It is not unusual to hear staff members speak to foreign visitors in their native languages — as the visitors learn from us, so too do we learn from them.

The Shakers spent their evenings in prayer meetings and organized interactions. When retiring for the night, the Sisters and Brothers climbed separate sets of stairs. Wide hallways prevented casual contact and opposite sides of the halls provided the sleeping rooms for the separated sexes. Some visitors occasionally find this celibate lifestyle unimaginable, yet records show that there was seldom a falling from grace. The system of order and Millennial Laws were so complete and the believers were so instilled with their faith that such problems seldom arose. Believers sometimes left the community to get married or simply because the Society wasn't right for them, but the Shakers who remained put their faith above worldly desires.

One interpreter told me a story about two Shakers who decided to leave to be married and their community reportedly gave them $500 to get started. This hardly speaks harshly of the Shakers' attitudes toward marriage. After all, without marriage of the "world's people," where would the Society find its converts? I have heard the Sisters talk of their desire to have families, but in the end, the family of the Shakers proved to be enough.

Evening after evening I reflected on the lives and times of these people. The last vestiges of daylight seemed to linger longer here than any other place I have been. As the special Believers kept journals and diaries, I attempted to keep a daily journal of my feelings and experiences. The Shakers seldom created art work, except for the inspired Spirit Drawings done during a period of spiritual renewal in the 1840s. Unlike the Shakers, I tried to capture everything on paper. Now, looking back through my journal, I find reflective entries that weave products and people in a written tapestry.

Weaving Area of the Sister's Shop at Hancock

It was in this setting that I began to re-create baskets

in the tradition of the Shakers. I carefully use the word "re-create" rather than "reproduce"; I wanted to feel the excitement of discovery rather than the chore of copying. The antique forms fascinated me when I first viewed them, even though moulded baskets were not new to me. In fact, the wide use of moulds by production basketmakers was rather common in New England. Moreover, a bushel basket had better hold a bushel, so the best way to be sure was to form it around a bushel-sized mould. It was these simple blocks of

Fancy sewing basket

Cat head basket

Quatrefoil design in fancy twilled tub

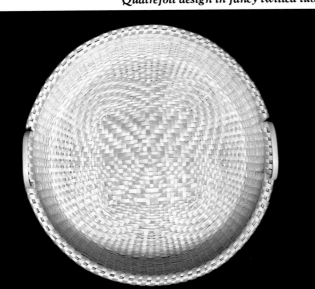

Double handled work basket

wood and their elegant shapes that really put me in touch with the Shakers and I chose to re-create those shapes that were unfamiliar to me.

A basket's basic shape is revealed by the mould, but how can one be sure of height, fineness of weave, or which handles to attach? Dozens of splint baskets were created in a variety of ways, using just one mould or form. So I began to pass judgment, using the sensitivities I had absorbed: this one was fine but that handle was better. The successful combination of one variable with another finally gave me the feeling for what the Shakers would have produced.

The summer continued to be a learning experience and one after another the number of re-creations grew. After all, from nearly 80 styles of Shaker baskets, variations on a theme came easily. Finally, I completed a repertoire of styles that continues to grow to this day.

During my stay at Hancock, a great joy was being able to fell black ash trees left behind by the Brothers because they were too small. These now mature trees at Hancock add their special quality to the forms that I make.

Fancy Shaker basket   *Bottom woven on a Watervliet mould*

Fancy twilled tub. (Baskets in this chapter handmade by John McGuire)

The basket industry.

The Shakers learned basketry partly from friendly

Algonquin Indians who lived nearby and acted as trading partners. The Shakers took the simple basket, elevated it to an art form and used it to generate a large dollar income for the community.

It is evident from reading about this industry that both women and men were involved. The woodworking aspects seemed to be the major task of the men although records indicate that men also wove baskets. It wasn't until men failed to join in sufficient numbers to keep various industries going that the Sisters began to do certain tasks rather than sacrifice those industries. Because basketry didn't require much male support to keep it going, it thrived longer than many other industries.

In researching Shaker basketry, the name of Daniel Boler comes up. As a young boy, this Believer came from Kentucky with his father. The two travelled to New Lebanon and remained there as members of the Church. As Daniel grew, his talents and mechanical abilities seemed to center around the basket industry and his involvement continued even after he was elevated to the Ministry in the Church family.

I have read interesting accounts describing the use of "twilling" in some Shaker baskets. Twilling was a technique in which the basketmaker produced a beautiful surface design by weaving "over and under two," or a variation of this technique. By doing this in a sequential order the basketmaker created a pattern, frequently on a diagonal. Shaker records reveal that most of these decorative baskets were made in New Lebanon, although some examples are found in Maine. It is thought that one person did the more complicated twill while another person with less ability did the regular weaving.

Sister Cornelia French (1840-1917), a native of Albany, New York, is apparently responsible for most of the twilled baskets and according to the records, she began making baskets at the age of 13 and produced them from 1855 to 1873 with some examples recorded in 1897. She lived and worked in the New Lebanon Church Family until she died at the age of 77. Eldress Harriet Goodwin (1823-1903) was also skilled in the decorative twill weave. The records do not reveal why Eldress Harriet was sent to Alfred, Maine from her Church Family in New Lebanon, but it is possible that she may have shared her technique with the Sisters in Maine.

Shaker made round field basket

Rectangular Shaker basket

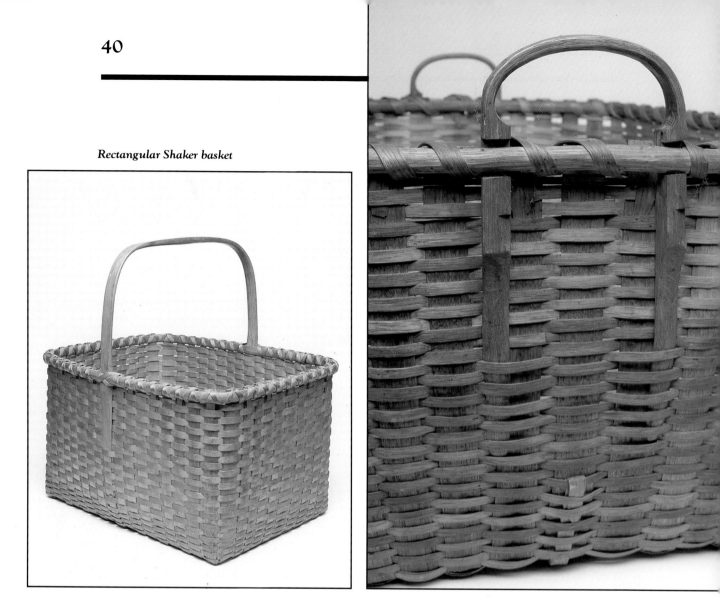

Note carved handles on laundry basket

Unusual four-handled Shaker basket from Canterbury, N.H.

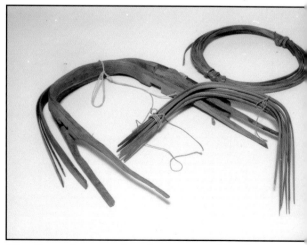

*Handles and weavers have been prepared in advance
for baskets made in a production mode.*

The Sisters produced most of the baskets, while the Brothers provided the support for this industry. Support involved preparation of the raw materials, the manufacture of basket handles, and other woodworking processes that guaranteed efficient production and high output. The wooden mould, of which there are dozens, attest to the variety of styles produced and score lines on individual moulds show the various possible heights of basket sides. A simple change in handle style and a new basket emerged, frequently named and sold according to its shape. Names were important for identification so that reorders could be filled efficiently and accurately.

As time passed, sales indicated consumer preference for smaller "fancy" baskets. The Shakers responded to this "trend" and decided to let the worldly producers make the bigger and plainer items. Besides, the smaller fancy baskets didn't deplete their ash supplies as rapidly and even the hexagonal "cheese baskets" or "curd baskets" took small amounts of splint. All of these smaller baskets required less masculine labor support and given the fact that the male population was shrinking, this became an important factor.

Ash splint Shaker basket

Shaker basket used for dining utensils

Shaker rectangular basket

Large Canterbury apple basket

The Trustees made market contacts and developed outlets for these items; it was not uncommon to find a traveling show selling Shaker wares set up in a hotel lobby. The Shakers astutely realized that if they were to compete, they needed to bring their finer, more special items to a public that could afford them — those who could pay to travel and stay at hotels. They also sold to wholesale buyers who widely distributed Shaker wares and fancy baskets and thus enriched Shaker industries. The word fancy today refers to intricate or dressy, while Shaker baskets were frequently both, the label refers to a high quality product.

Canterbury apple basket

Shaker cat head basket

Round basket with carved initials

Utility basket

The basket industry.

While some fancy basketmaking lasted into the 20th century, this production was very spotty and sales were augmented with Native American and German imports that met the high standards of the Shakers. Some of these German imports had dark colored accents, and the use of a few strands of indigo-dyed splints as a decorative aspect began to appear in Shaker work. This recent fancy basketry was made entirely in the Sisters' shop and did not involve the more diversified areas that had once contributed production to this industry.

The impact of the veneering machine, which was developed to produce basket splint in the 1850s, was felt greatly by "worldly" basketmakers, but seemed to have little immediate effect on the Shakers. The "worldly" maker couldn't compete and fell victim to industrial technology. The Shakers were more fortunate in that baskets were not their only source of revenue. What really crippled Shaker basketry and their other industries was the decline in numbers of men needed to support those industries.

Shaker basket with CB label

Early Shaker basket

Large black ash basket

Rectangular utility basket

Antique tools and technology.

After learning the basic techniques from nearby

Native Americans, Yankees, and other basketmakers, the Believers soon turned basket-making into an industry. The raw materials existed on their own properties and the Shakers also owned land in the Adirondacks which continued to provide ash after the local supply dwindled.

The bark of the black ash (*Fraxinus nigra*) was pulled off with a bark spud. Made by the blacksmith, this item had a stout curved blade and wooden handle. The sharpened blade, which reflected the curve of the log, helped peel the bark off black ash and other logs. The bark of these trees was used to produce tannin for the tanning industry, which was operated by the Shakers into the second half of the 19th century. Typical of good business people, the Shakers attempted to dovetail industries and make wide use of interrelated technologies.

Rectangular and spoon basket moulds

Cat head mould

Large basket mould

After removing the bark, the splints were prepared. Native Algonquins, who helped teach the Shakers, prepared splints by hand, using a wooden club to pound the annual growth rings off. Once the Shakers harnessed running water to supply the power, they built a triphammer to beat the logs and loosen ash strips. This hammer was also used by the blacksmith to pound out metal and to break flax. It was a rather simple machine — a device pulled up a weighted head to a specified height, then a release mechanism dropped this weight or hammer head on the log. It was a great labor-saving device that efficiently produced large quantities of splints.

Another device was the froe that helped split out wood for handles and rims or billets of ash for pounding. (A billet was a narrow width of ash, many growth rings thick, which could be fed more efficiently into a triphammer.) Other essentials were knives for cleaning and carving. Native Americans used a crooked knife which was frequently made out of a straight razor. The Shakers forged their own knives and utensils or had them made elsewhere. There was also a device that thinned materials to a uniform thickness; its rollers allowed the splint to be pulled through easily and tension screws adjusted the pressure on

Multiple handle mould

*Billet of ash
showing delamination of
growth rings by pounding*

Kitten head moulds

Deep fancy mould

Miniature moulds

Splint plane

the splint as it rolled over a sharpened blade, thus controlling the amount of excess that was removed.

A very necessary tool was used to cut or slit the splint into narrow strips — a few of the more common slitters are shown here. They were used to cut straw and palm leaf for hats and bonnets, and more refined versions were later used to prepare poplar wood for basketry and poplarware. Powered by various means, all slitters or cutters had a series of fine blades that cut multiples of uniformly wide weavers or uprights.

Perhaps the most important element in Shaker basketry was the use of moulds or forms of almost unlimited varieties. The photographs here represent just a few. The handle forms enabled the basketmaker to bend dozens at one time. Basket templates were also employed to standardize sizes and improve production.

Of course, the Shakers also used scissors, saws, and clamps for obvious reasons. Other critical tools were the shavehorse and the drawknife. The shavehorse was nothing more than a clamp to hold the wood, so both hands were free to use a drawknife. The drawknife consisted of a blade with a handle at either end; it was used to carve the piece of wood held in the jaws of the shavehorse.

Straw slitters used in bonnet making

Oval mould with supports

Puzzle mould, completely reconstructed from Hancock remnant (left), disassembles into three parts to release basket.

For someone who wishes to make Shaker baskets, it

can be easy to accumulate a variety of tools. Actually, the number of tools needed are very few: a good jackknife, a piece of canvas or leather to cover your knee, some scissors, clamps or clothespins, a small saw, a pencil, and perhaps a tape measure.

Spray bottles can be used to keep the wood splints damp and increment borers are handy should you wish to test a tree before cutting. Soaking tanks, PVC pipes, or other water-holding devices will keep materials pliable and a "worldly" microwave oven will heat up wet wood for bending in seconds. Other optional tools include: the froe, dividing box, slitting gauge, drawknife, shavehorse, mallet, and awl.

The Shakers were able to produce baskets in commercial quantities because of their use of moulds. A number of these moulds are included in this book to illustrate their variety. If you decide to make your own moulds out of wood, as the originals were, or from resins or other materials, refer to the photographs for the correct shape. A limited selection of moulds and other tools is available from suppliers listed in the back of this book.

It is important to keep your tools sharp. Nothing wears down enthusiasm more than a dull tool, so do buy a whetstone; it can be the type that uses water as the

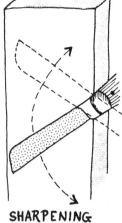

SHARPENING PATTERN

lubricant, or the more traditional oil stone. (Oil stones frequently become clogged with oil; bake them in a moderate oven for about 15-20 minutes to remedy this situation.) The real key to sharpening tools is to hold the knife at a shallow angle; slightly lift the back of the blade off the stone in a 10° angle. Keeping the edge in maximum contact with the stone, draw the blade across the stone and away from you. Turn the blade over and reverse the motion (this arc will move toward your hand, but the back of the blade is heading toward your fingers). To prevent accidents, do not arc the cutting edge toward you — leave this technique up to the experts. Continue until the blade is sharp and then polish the edge on a piece of leather. The same technique is used for drawknives as well, however the contoured edge is the only one sharpened. Always be careful!

Finally, a most important tool is your own creativity. If you don't want a shavehorse in your living room, just invent another way to clamp the wood. "Where there is a will, there is a way." Be creative!

The black ash tree.

The black ash (*Fraxinus nigra*) is the northernmost native ash tree and is so named because of its dark brown heartwood. This particular tree has a number of nicknames: basket ash, basket tree, hoop ash, and brown ash, to name a few. Black ash trees are found in the wet soils of cold swamps and peat bogs where drainage is poor and also along the boundaries of coniferous and hardwood forests. It is found at all altitudes up to 3,500 feet in the areas southeast of Manitoba and east to Newfoundland, as far south as West Virginia, and as far west as Iowa.

Ecological changes and other conditions are threatening the black ash trees' existence. Beaver dams cause water to back up, thereby producing dangerous stagnant conditions, yet young trees ironically seem to sense the danger and produce bountiful seedlings. If you find the remnants of black ash in one area, look downwind of the prevailing winds – re-establishment is probable.

Because of their habitat, black ash trees are rarely more than one foot in diameter. Their strong branches show a distinct absence of small twigs or branches. The center stem of the leaf structure provides a stalk from which the broad, slightly serrated leaves grow without a lead stem. When losing leaves, it sheds this entire structure and sets blue-black buds that sprout in the spring. The prolific seeds hang in clusters and mature in late summer.

Perhaps the most distinctive identifying feature of the black ash is the bark. (See photos on pages 142 & 143.) Frequently it resembles that of elm, but it is far more corky and, when rubbed, the scaly plates flake off easily. Only moderate fissures characterize this bark, whereas pronounced fissures and a rugged bark are characteristic of the white ash. Two sure giveaways are the leaf structure (white ash has a lead stem and black ash does not) and the fact that white ash dislikes wet soils. White ash does prepare similarly and can be used as an alternate source for splint, but it is less supple and is more difficult to handle during the pounding process.

Because of the decline in numbers of black ash trees due to its popularity for basketmaking and its limited growing range, other woods, including white oak and hickory, were often substituted. The preparation of those woods requires strong hands and requires splitting out the rings for baskets. Referred to as "splits," this terminology seems most prevalent in the south where black ash does not grow and is replaced by other woods, most notably white oak.

Recently the black ash has been regaining its traditional growing range as immature trees

have had time to re-seed and re-establish themselves. Should you choose to use this uniquely distinctive wood to make your baskets, your work will not fail to win appreciation. Black ash imparts its unique color and character to baskets and its workable nature also makes it possible to cut the finest of weavers without sacrificing strength in the finished basket.

The first rule of thumb, when selecting a black ash tree, is to secure permission from the appropriate landowners. The Shakers were fortunate to have vast landholdings which provided them with the abundant ash their basketry industry required. Because they heated with wood, they also were skilled woodsmen and were accomplished at felling trees. Few of us are skilled in selecting and felling trees, so it is essential to locate someone with experience.

Once you find a stand of black ash, be selective! Don't let your enthusiasm cloud your judgment. A straight, knot-free trunk at least six feet tall is the minimum you should consider cutting; a ten to twelve foot tree is best. If you'd prefer not to fell your own black ash tree, refer to the supplier resource list at the back of this book.

Use of an increment borer (available from a forester) will mean a better selection. With this device, you can remove a small plug without killing the tree and study the internal rings and their thicknesses. Because adverse growing conditions are reflected in the rings, you can avoid felling a bad tree. Should you have to depend on your wits, select a tree that has all the optimum growing conditions. Cut a tree which has no blemish marks in the trunk, and try to remove as much of the tree as possible or at least cut up the unwanted portions and scatter them to encourage its return to the soil. Leave the area as neat and untouched as possible.

Once your tree is at home, cover it with leaves or coat the ends to prevent loss of moisture (Native Americans coated their logs with mud to prevent drying). Try to pound the log for splint as soon as possible or else keep it soaked in a pond or some tank. I have experienced little problem in pounding trees taken down at any time of the year, but fully saturated logs found in the spring are the easiest to work. Should your tree be stubborn, soaking will probably help and frequent ladling of water onto the log during the pounding process makes the job easier.

If you purchase a tree, the exchange of a basket for the tree has been a long-standing tradition. In fact, this exchange — a basket for a tree — gave the "basket tree" one of its nicknames.

Preparation of black ash splint.

Once you have removed the bark with a bark spud or some other device, you need to begin the pounding as quickly as possible. Elevate the log to facilitate pounding and to maximize impact. Using the end grain of a wooden mallet, begin to pound, overlapping each blow. At the beginning, repeat each strike, to hasten the loosening of the layers or growth rings. Usually the first day's pounding will produce very little splint, but the results of subsequent days will benefit from your initial day of endless drudgery. The important thing to remember is to let the weight of the mallet create the impact. If you drive the blow, you can damage your tendons and nerves. Instead, relax your wrist at the moment of impact and let the mallet do the work.

Do not hurry the pounding process. Unusually harsh pounding can fracture the wood and make the splint nearly worthless. Consistent and repetitive blows are better for freeing the splint from other layers.

You may find that your log has experienced drought conditions or some other type of deprivation. If this has occurred, paper-thin layers of splint are often the result and these are frequently too fragile to be used. Considerable time can be saved if you remove these layers with a drawknife.

Once it is completely removed from the log, you will notice the wide range of colors found in the splint. The rich darker brown splint closer to the center is wonderful —students frequently use this wood in combination with the lighter-colored outer sapwood to pattern a basket. However, this color variation is a temporary condition and aging will produce an overall darkening that will negate your patterning efforts. If you wish to produce color variations, walnut hulls can be used to produce a beautiful permanent dye.

Select 5-8 lengths of splint of similar quality or thickness and coil them together in a bundle. Then, whenever you need a particular quality or thickness, you can go to that bundle.

Once I select the coil to be used for a particular basket, I can resoak it in water almost indefinitely. However, minor decomposition can occur and a scum is produced, but this film is easily washed away. Sometimes decomposition causes a darkening of the splint,

which some find appealing and antique-looking; this decomposition can be slowed down by using water mixed with bleach or swimming pool chemicals, to reduce bacterial growth.

The reason I choose the wet method of working is because it allows me to finish the entire preparatory process at one time. Using soaked (but not dripping wet) splint, I can cut it to more manageable widths and prepare it for the next step.

I then divide and subdivide the wet splint *before* I clean it, because subdivided splint is much more pliable and is frequently easier to clean. If a growth ring is exceptionally heavy, you may first halve it and then subdivide the halves (multiple subdivisions within one ring are quite possible).

Use moist splint that has been thoroughly soaked and score it with a sharp knife; then break the surface back by folding it in half. A natural tab forms; careful pulling on this tab will allow you to begin separation. Should this cut be too shallow, re-score and start again. Try to get this first division in the center so the splint divides in half. Once started, place the end of the splint between your legs and begin to peel down the center. Should the split division be off center, stop pulling on the thinner side and pull harder on the thicker. The tear or division should travel into the heavier section and back to center; you should be able to keep it there by peeling evenly on both halves. Remember that there are no lines or layers here; it is one solid piece of wood with the grain in one direction. If you simply pull, it will tear apart, so even tension and care are the keys to even division.

Some students develop their own style of dividing and it is amazing to see the variety of techniques that are possible. One sure-fire way is to construct a dividing box with an opening that fits the bulk of your splints without a lot of extra space. With the box held between the knees, a controlled pull *against its sides* does the dividing. Frequently the box accidently slips and the splint may be pulled up and out of the dividing area; without the support of the box, the splint then tears into pieces. It's important to pull out and *down* against the sides of the box.

Use either the box method or the hand method, not a combination of the two. They do not integrate well. Once you become proficient with the box, you will probably only use the hand method to divide the largest and most unmanageable pieces. Following are simple directions for constructing a dividing box. Should you have a vise, its open jaws can be used for the same purpose as a box.

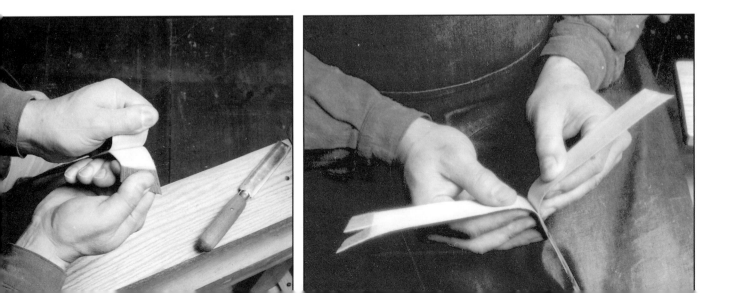

Constructing a dividing box.

Using two hardwood boards of the same length, cut a shallow groove one half the total depth you need (1/16″ to 3/32″ maximum) and approximately 2″ wide in both pieces. Splint wider than this is hard to separate and work with easily. Apply a heavy wax coating or finish to the slots, keeping it away from the edges. Glue the two boards together. Round the opening on one end to facilitate first divisions and keep the other end a sharp edge (this tighter radius will help in subdividing thinner materials).

Alternatively, take a single board and cut a deep lengthwise groove in the middle, creating a slot. Insert the splint and take care that it does not slide out the open side. Or, if you are a more accomplished woodworker, construct an adjustable dividing box using wing nuts and bolts that allow the throat to be opened or closed.

One note about commercial splint: wood splints are cut by veneering machines or a combination of machines that cut across the growth rings. These splints will not subdivide and are fairly fragile. Except for use in larger baskets, they are useless for Shaker work.

Cleaning the splints.

Cleaning is accomplished by flattening the moistened splint with the blade of your knife against a piece of leather placed on your thigh. The leather is there to protect your clothes and to act as a skid for the material to slide against when pulling it into the knife. The object is to clean the entire surface with an even motion. Hold the straight edge of the knife parallel to the splint and at a slight angle, to engage the hairy, woody fibers (cambium) with the edge of the knife. Exert a pressure against the splint that flattens it so the entire blade is in contact with the splint. Starting at one end, pull the splint toward you against the stationary knife blade with an even tug. The cambium should begin to clean off, leaving a smooth but dull surface. Cambium cleans off better in one direction than the other and the convex or outer surface cleans best. If cleaning is difficult, turn the strip around or play with the angle of the knife. Cleaning may also present difficulties if the splint is too wet. Keep your knife sharp and remember to hone the edge after sharpening. The concave side of the splint will be more difficult to clean, because these fibers are more recessed and will resist removal. Just do your best to clean as much as possible and use the best surface of the splint to be the outside of your basket.

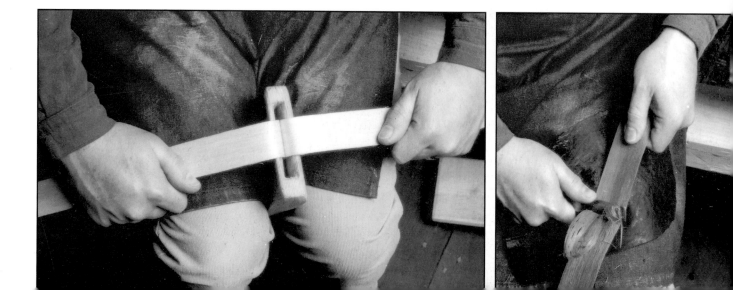

If you do not choose to clean splint using the wet method, you can scrape the surface with a paint scraper. In this case, lay the splint on a board and clean off the outer surface by removing the cambium layer, which adheres to the more dense ring. Do this carefully because gouging can weaken areas of the splint, making it a problem to subdivide it into thinner strips. For this reason, I recommend subdivision prior to cleaning, until a student becomes familiar with the process.

Sizing the weavers.

For nearly a year I used scissors to cut my weavers, but now I employ cutting gauges made from sharpened thin clocksprings set at desired intervals and glued and braced in position. I know Native American basketmakers who excel at making gauges, yet they still prefer to use a pair of sharp scissors. When using scissors, if you are right-handed, first straighten the left edge of your splint and then cut from left to right. Reverse if you are left-handed. The wisdom of this advice will become apparent right away because then the cutting line is visible and the width easier to control.

Gauges require strength to pull heavy material through the blades and so finer materials are frequently used with these aids. The photograph below illustrates the technique: hold the splint down with your thumb and pull down and against the blades in an even fashion. Jerky motions encourage splints to shift in the channel and throws the cutting off, giving you poor results.

Finally, make sure you prepare enough material, so you don't have to stop in the middle of a basket to prepare more. Any extra weavers can be stored easily and will be available for your next project.

Selecting material weight.

When you are ready to weave, pay attention to the weight of the material you are using. Unlike commercial materials, you can choose and control the weight of both the uprights and weavers. I find that weavers approximately 1/4 lighter in weight than the uprights prove to be the best rule of thumb. Too light a weaver and the body of the basket is weak; too heavy and they weaken or overpower the uprights and complicate proper shaping of the basket.

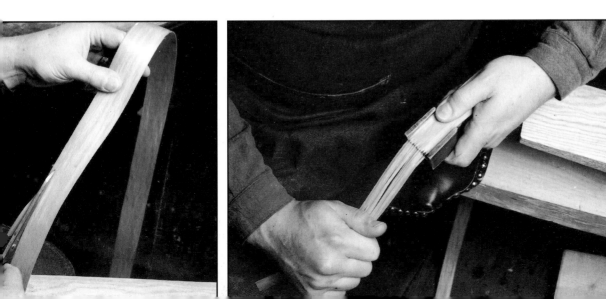

Making the baskets.

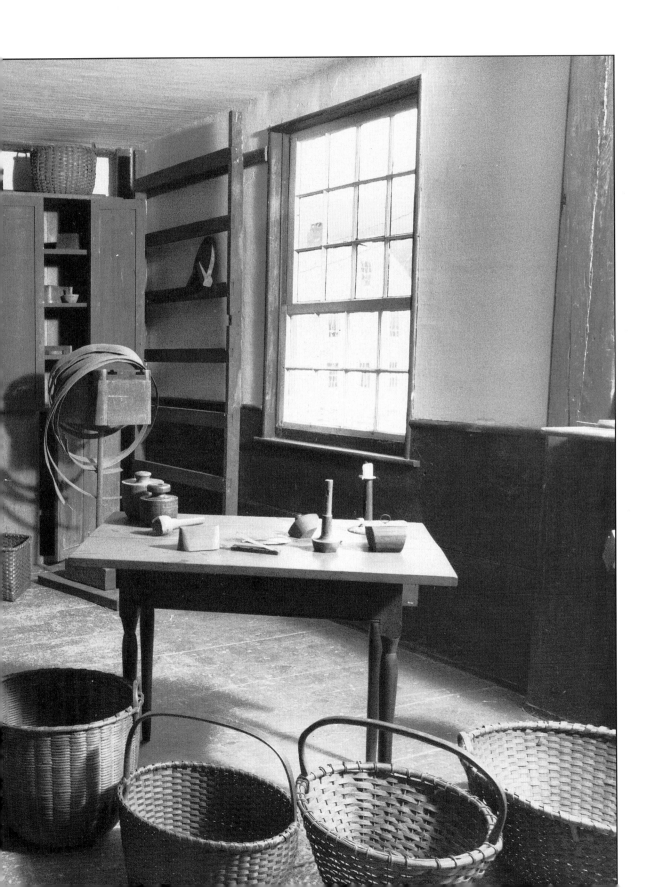

Making a cat head basket.

The cat head basket is probably one of the most recognized forms of Shaker fancy work. It gets its name from the shape — when the basket is turned over, the bottom resembles a cat's head.

I use a plastic mould instead of the more traditional wooden one, to illustrate that a plastic container can be used. This lightweight and non-absorbing mould allows the maker to resoak splint while it is still attached to the form, yet without damaging the mould. It also allows easy removal of the basket when it is done.

To start, place a sheet of plastic over the bottom of the mould. With a waterproof pen, mark the corners or ears of the mould. Now connect the points with a straight edge; this square is the maximum size your bottom should be (the one shown here measures 3½" square). If the basket bottom exceeds this size, the ears or points will be distorted. Locate the center of this square; this is where you will begin the bottom.

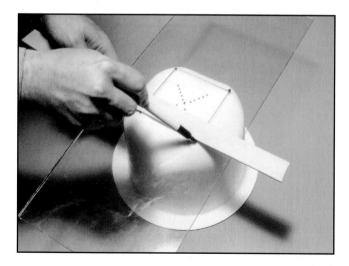

Measure the lengths of the uprights; an uneven number (9, in this case) is needed on both sides. This is a "square-to-round" basket and the odd number of uprights will allow the handle to be placed symmetrically in the basket. Our uprights are 16" long, giving an allowance of 1" on each side to fold over and tuck in when the weaving is

done. (The mould is taller than the finished basket to allow for this extra allowance.) Our grid or bottom pattern will accommodate 18 uprights, approximately ¼" wide.

Start weaving the bottom out from the center. Weave with the best side of all material showing up, as this surface will be the outside of your basket. Add uprights in a symmetrical fashion noting the space used by each addition. If the 3½" bottom is filling up too quickly, tighten up the spaces by sliding the ribs closer together. In the basket shown here, I started with three parallel uprights at the center. I then added a perpendicular upright and then uprights to the left and right of the starting point. I then built out symmetrically in all directions.

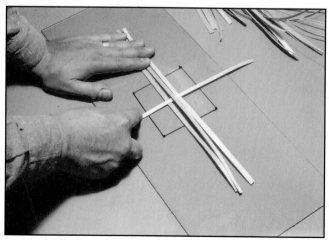

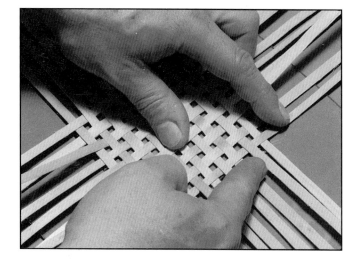

Once all the uprights are woven in, check to be sure that you haven't exceeded the corners. Try to stay slightly inside of the bottom pattern to allow for the addition of a "keeper." Starting halfway over the top of an upright and near the midpoint of one side, weave in this fine (1/16″ or less) locking strip to prevent the bottom from shifting. At the corners, fold the keeper to form it neatly; this folded or mitered corner is only done with the keeper. I've used a colored keeper here to clearly illustrate this step.

Continue to weave in the keeper, making sure the corners are neatly formed. Once you return to the starting point, overlap the two ends for a distance of four ribs and conceal the joint under a rib.

Placing thumb and fingers into the four corners, put the basket bottom on the reproduction mould. Close your eyes if necessary and feel the points of the mould with your fingers and thumbs to assure proper positioning. Drill several holes in the mould that will line up with the open spaces in the basket bottom.

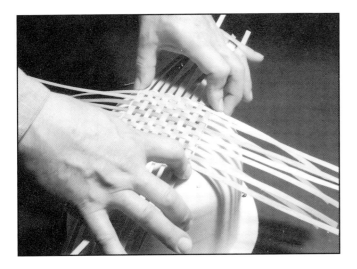

Secure the bottom to the mould by placing a rubber washer against the basket and a metal washer on top of the rubber one. Put a thumbscrew into the washer hole and secure a wing nut to the inside, tightening the bottom to the mould. Be sure the bottom is secured well enough to the mould to prevent the bottom from shifting off the corners as you proceed (in the photo here, I've also used a rivet with a large head to keep the bottom from shifting).

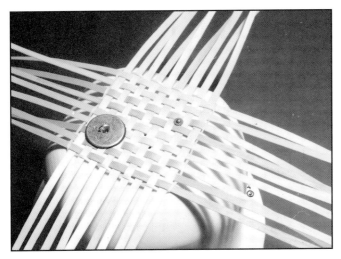

Select a weaver to begin weaving the sides. Weaving splints should be slightly lighter in weight than the uprights and should be very narrow (approximately 3/32″) in order to re-create a Shaker

appearance. Starting about 1/3 of the distance from an end, taper the weaver a distance of two inches with sharp scissors until you have gradually reduced the width to a thread-like appearance. Now begin to widen the taper, returning it to full width.

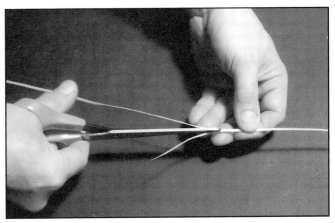

Weaving this basket will use a method called "chasing," which allows the use of two weavers at one time. Start at a corner and weave in a start weaver for a short distance. Weave from the middle of the tapered section and make sure its best side

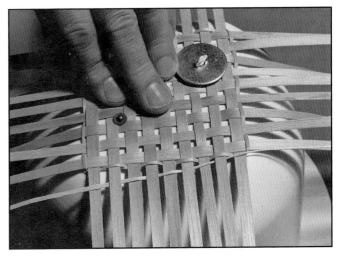

is showing. Now fold under the rest of the weaver and loop it under the rib that you began on. If there is a bad or rougher side showing, twist the weaver to place the best side out. Don't worry about the twist showing; it is so small and only done once, so it is nearly undetectable.

Now weave in the reversed weaver; the photograph shows that you are now going over what you went under on the second upright. At this point you have two weavers heading in the same direction; this allows you to weave faster and without splitting an upright. You will weave this basket with two weavers until finished.

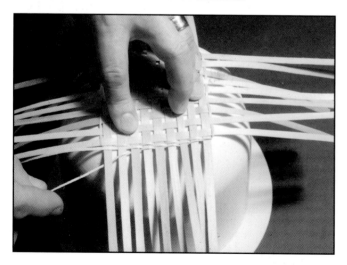

Refer to the picture to make sure your pattern is correct. Always keep your weavers pushed down snugly against each other so that gaps are prevented and the material is kept as close to the mould as possible. Pulling the weavers tight is not necessary; simply weave in the material and press the upright against the mould to prevent the basket from lifting off the mould. Let the mould do the work of shaping.

When forming the corners or ears, pull the corner uprights together and weave around the corner; repeat with the second weaver.

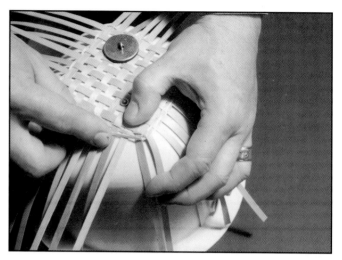

In the photograph below it is apparent that the ears are beginning to form and pull slightly away from the mould. The tapered beginning section has now been reached and you can see how well-concealed the starting point becomes. If the corners drift out of position, use a misting bottle to dampen them. Be sure that the weavers are not crushed at the corners; if they are compacting or crushing, the weavers are too flimsy.

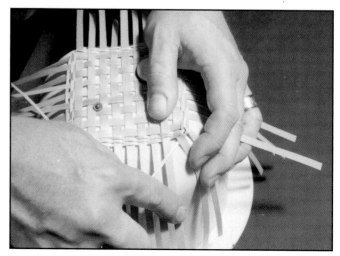

Do not add new weavers at the corners, at least not until you have formed the ears and are well into the upper portion of the basket. When you're close to running out of a weaver, stop either before or after finishing a corner. Blunt cut the end of the weaver and position it in the middle and on top of an upright. Starting at this upright, count back four uprights (if correct, you will be at an upright that has a weaver going under it).

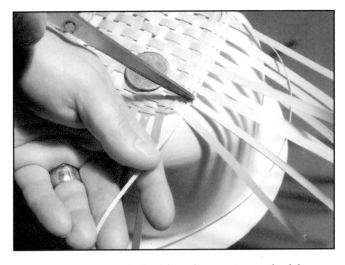

Tuck the blunt beginning end of the new weaver under this fourth upright and directly on top of the weaver which is already in place. Weave over the top of this earlier weaver and continue on lapping over the top of the cut end of the old weaver.

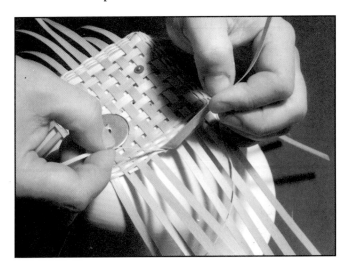

Continue to weave as before. Adding all weavers in this way gives extra strength and prevents unsightly tails from being seen.

You will be weaving with two strips throughout, but only the first is narrowed and folded back on itself. The others are joined to the two ends of the start weaver as described above. The Shakers frequently thinned their splint at the joins to remove bumps caused by overlapping ends. You may choose to do this in your baskets to improve their looks.

If you press the upright you are about to weave over against the mould and then exert a minimal pull, you weave the rib against the mould better. Not all areas will conform perfectly to the mould; the ears will float away a bit.

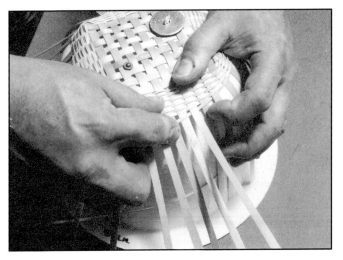

This round basket started with a square bottom, but once the ears are formed you must begin to position the uprights equidistant from each other so as to make the basket round.

Shaping progresses in the next photograph, showing that some drift away from the mould is permissible. In some Shaker baskets that have less pronounced ears, the weaving conforms to the mould more completely. Keep the weavers snug to each other, because it will be difficult to tighten this area later. Frequent misting and occasional pulling the upright down and against the sides of the mould as you weave will improve the basket's shape.

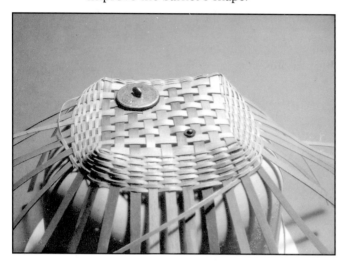

Once you have completed the chase weave, stop about 1″ short of the tops of the uprights. This is done to allow the addition of a false rim (about the width of the uprights) and still leave enough for folding over the rim and tucking the upright ends back into the weaving.

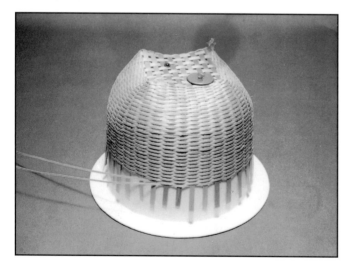

To end, cut the two weavers near the same corner where you began to weave. Clip them so the ends are behind an upright and clip the top weaver behind the lower one, so as to stagger the ends and conceal the ending point. It is quite noticeable if both weavers stop at the same place.

Remove the basket from the mould and taper the ends of the weavers. Allow the basket to dry completely — a full day is necessary. The bottom photograph shows the tapered ending and how much tightening or downward packing of the weavers is

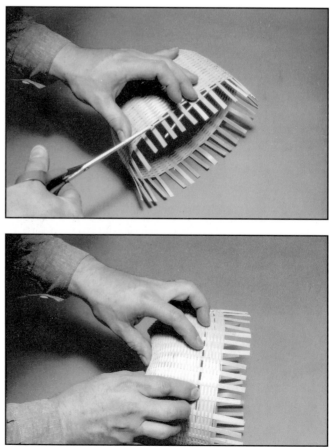

necessary after the basket dries. Because the basket will shrink as it dries, you may want to weave it higher than desired, to compensate for this shrinkage. Careful use of a microwave oven can hasten the drying process, without destroying the resiliency of the wood. Dry the basket a few times at a controlled low setting.

The addition of a false rim allows the lashing and the inner and outer rims to be secured to this band and eliminates having to lash into the weavers, which throws off the level of the basket. Begin weaving in a strip of splint the width of the anticipated rim (often the same width as the uprights). Start with the false rim halfway over the top of an upright and weave it in, taking note of the weaving pattern below. At the areas where you ended your weavers you are going to alter the weaving so as to "lock" in as much of these weavers as possible. In my basket, because of the distances between my staggered ending weavers, I will have to adjust the weaving pattern twice by "floating over" the ribs where I ended the two weavers. The loose tapered ends of the ending weavers can be simply caught in the final lashing process, thereby securing them. The photograph below clearly shows how these adjustments are made twice. Should you end the weavers very close to each other, only one adjustment may be necessary.

In ending the false rim, float over the beginning point (which can be nearly anywhere) and weave over the top of the lower false rim for a distance of four uprights; cut and secure the end behind the fourth rib. Blunt point or point the ends of the ribs that stick up beyond the false rim and soak them to make them pliable by setting the basket upside down in a shallow pan of water. Do not resoak the whole basket.

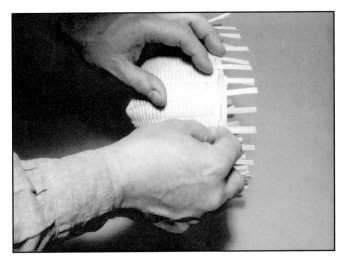

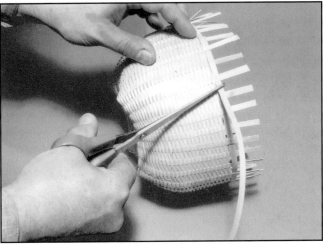

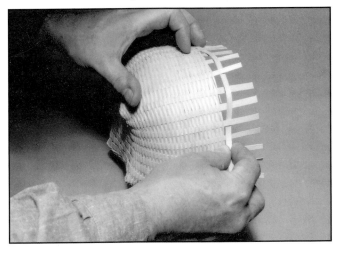

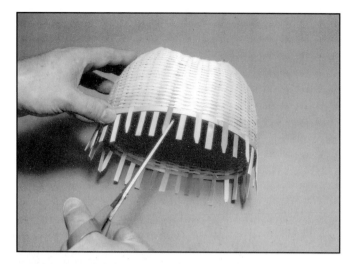

Score any ribs that are too thick to fold over easily with a shallow cut and peel back the excess. Fold the ends of the pointed ribs over the false rim and secure them into the weaving. An awl or other tool will help you open the spaces for the tucked ends. Cut off all remaining uprights so they are even with the false rim.

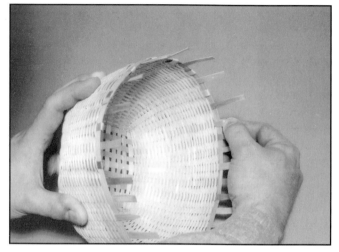

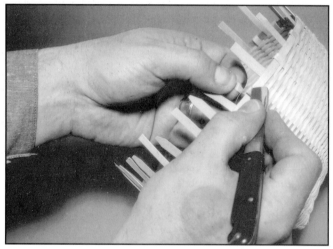

This basket is so named because its shape is somewhat reminiscent of the shape of the bowl of a spoon. The mould shown here is an exact replica of the one at Hancock Shaker Village Museum. It is $4\frac{1}{2}''$ wide, $6''$ long, and $3\frac{1}{2}''$ high. Its shape can be sculpted with wood putty.

This basket will use the same weight uprights and weavers as in the Cat Head basket. However, an even number of uprights (12, in this case) will be used on the sides because there is no handle to be inserted. Uprights should be cut at least $1''$ longer on each end, for folding over a false rim.

For the basket ends use an uneven number (9, in this case) of lengthwise uprights that are $\frac{1}{4}''$ wide and $15''$ long. An uneven number is needed so that the handles, which span three uprights, can be centered. Next, cut the 12 uprights for the basket sides to a length of $13\frac{1}{2}''$. This length is a total of the $4\frac{1}{2}''$ basket width plus the two side heights of $3\frac{1}{2}''$ plus the $1''$ for each end to fold and tuck over the rim.

To start, place a sheet of plastic over the bottom of the mould. (You may also use any other material which enables you to locate the corner of the bottom.) With a waterproof pen, mark the corners of the mould. Remove the plastic sheet and connect the points with a straight edge; this is the maximum size your bottom should be. Locate the center; this is where you will begin the bottom.

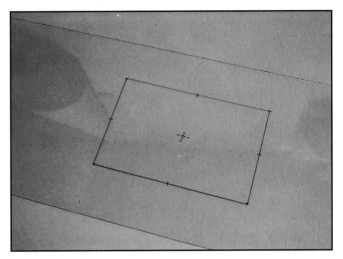

Start weaving the bottom out from the center. Weave with the best side of all material showing up, as this surface will be the outside of the basket.

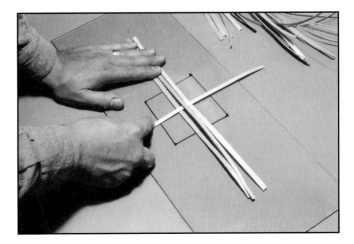

Add uprights in a symmetrical fashion and then fill the ends, noting the space used by each addition. If the bottom pattern is filling up too quickly, tighten up the spaces by sliding the ribs closer together. Try to stay slightly inside of the bottom pattern to allow for the addition of a "keeper."

Starting halfway over the top of an upright and near the midpoint of one side, weave in a fine ($1/16''$ or less) locking strip to prevent the bottom from shifting. At the corners, fold the keeper (colored here for clarity) to form it neatly; this folded or mitered corner is only done with the keeper. Continue to weave in the keeper, making sure the corners are neatly formed. Once you return to the starting point, overlap the two ends for a distance of four ribs and conceal the joint under a rib.

Place the base onto the mould and pin or nail it securely in place. Be sure the bottom is secured well enough to the mould to prevent the bottom from shifting as you proceed.

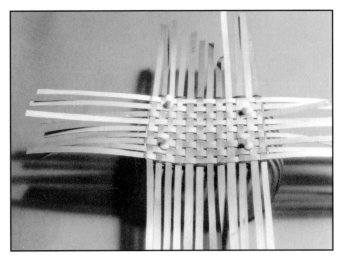

This view shows the entire working position. I have drilled the bottom of the wooden mold and have elevated it on a post so as to weave more conveniently.

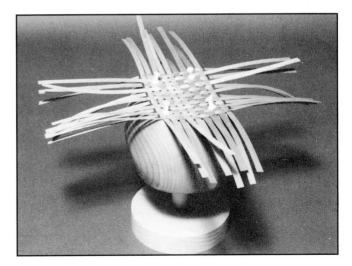

Select a weaver to begin weaving the sides. Weaving splints should be slightly lighter in weight than the uprights and should be very narrow (approximately 3/32″) in order to re-create a Shaker appearance. Starting about 1/3 of the distance from an end, taper the weaver a distance of 2″ with sharp scissors until you have gradually reduced the width to a thread-like appearance. Now begin to widen the taper, returning it to full width.

Weaving this basket will use a method called "chasing," which allows the use of two weavers at one time. Start at a corner and use the hourglass shaped weaver just created. Weave from the middle of the tapered section and make sure its best side

is showing. Now fold under the rest of the weaver and loop it under the rib that you began on. If there is a bad or rougher side showing, twist the weaver to place the best side out. Don't worry, about the twist showing; it is so small and only done once, so it is nearly undetectable.

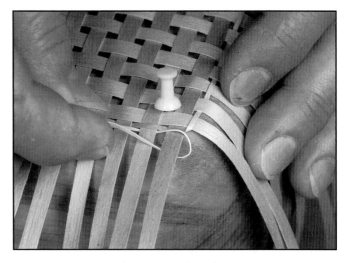

Now weave in the reversed weaver. You are now going over what you went under on the second upright. At this point you have two weavers heading in the same direction; this allows you to weave faster and without splitting an upright. You will weave this basket with two weavers until finished as we did with the cat head basket.

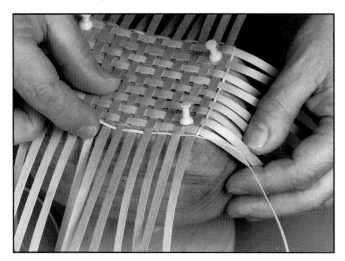

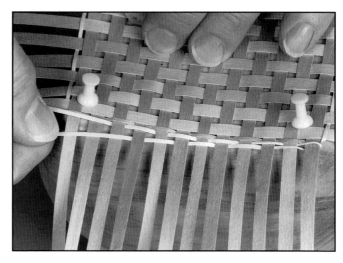

Refer to the picture to make sure your pattern is correct. Always keep your weavers pushed down snugly against each other so that gaps are prevented and the material is kept as close to the mould as possible. Pulling the weavers tight is not necessary; simply weave in the material and press the upright against the mould to prevent the basket from lifting off the mould. Let the mould do the work of shaping.

When you're close to running out of a weaver, blunt cut the end of the weaver and position it in the middle and on top of an upright. Starting at this upright, count back four uprights (if correct, you will be at an upright that has a weaver going under it).

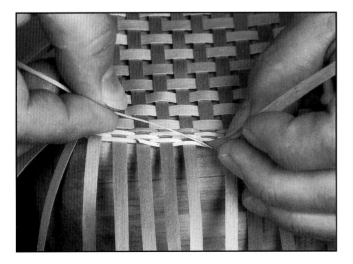

Tuck the blunt cut beginning end of a new weaver under this fourth upright and directly on top of the weaver which is already in place. Weave over the top of this earlier weaver and continue on, lapping over the top of the cut end of the old weaver. Adding all weavers in this way gives extra strength and prevents unsightly tails from being seen.

You will be weaving with two strips throughout, but only the first is narrowed and folded back on itself. The others are joined to the two ends of the start weaver as described above. The Shakers frequently thinned their splint at the joins to remove bumps caused by overlapping ends. You may choose to do this in your baskets to improve their looks.

Keep the weavers snug to each other, because it will be difficult to tighten them later. Frequent misting and occasional pulling the upright down and against the sides of the mould as you weave will improve the basket's shape. Remember to fan out the uprights evenly when weaving to help shape the basket.

If you do not wish to chase weave, simply choose an upright with care and split it. Do not split an upright at the corners as this will alter the look and the position of the handle.

Once you have completed the chase weave, stop about 1″ short of the tops of the uprights. This is done to allow the addition of a false rim (about the width of the uprights) and still leave enough for folding over the rim and tucking the upright ends back into the weaving.

To end, cut the two weavers near the same corner where you began to weave. Clip them so the ends are behind an upright and clip the top weaver behind the lower one, so as to stagger the ends and conceal the ending point. It is quite noticeable if both weavers stop at the same place.

Because our mold turns inward at the top, it is easier to remove the basket if you stop before reaching the full height. I suggest you weave the last few rows freehand. If you weave extra tight to this or any mold, you can facilitate the basket's removal by placing the mold and the weaving in a freezer for a short while.

The Shakers frequently created puzzle molds which broke apart, enabling the maker to remove the basket with ease.

Remove the basket from the mould and taper the ends of the weavers. Allow the basket to dry completely - a full day is necessary. The bottom photograph shows the tapered ending and how much tightening or downward packing of the weavers is necessary after the basket dries. Because the

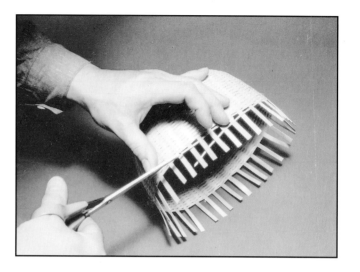

basket will shrink as it dries, you may want to weave it higher than desired, to compensate for this shrinkage. Careful use of a microwave oven can hasten the drying process, without destroying the resiliency of the wood. Dry the basket a few times at a controlled low setting.

The addition of a false rim allows the lashing and the inner and outer rims to be secured to this band and eliminates having to lash into the weavers, which throws off the level of the basket. Begin weaving in a strip of splint the width of the anticipated rim (often the same width as the uprights). Start with the false rim halfway over the top of an upright and weave it in taking note of the weaving pattern below. At the areas where you ended your weavers you are going to alter the weaving so as to "lock" in as much of these weavers as possible. The loose tapered ends of the ending weavers can be simply caught in the final lashing process, thereby securing them.

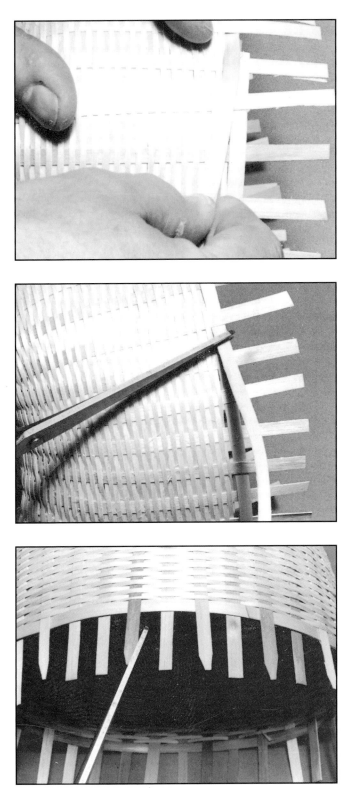

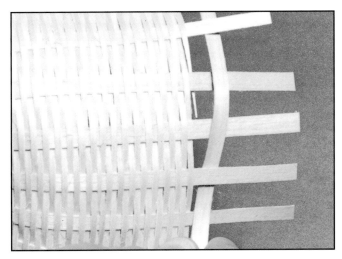

In ending the false rim, float over the beginning point (which can be nearly anywhere) and weave over the top of the lower false rim for a distance of four uprights; cut and secure the end behind the fourth rib. Blunt point or point the ends of the ribs that stick up beyond the false rim and soak them to make them pliable by setting the basket upside down in a shallow pan of water. Do not resoak the whole basket.

Score any ribs that are too thick to fold over easily with a shallow cut and peel back the excess. Fold the ends of the pointed ribs over the false rim and secure them into the weaving. An awl or other tool will help you open the spaces for the tucked ends. Cut off all remaining uprights so they are even with the false rim.

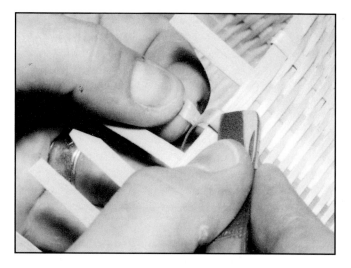

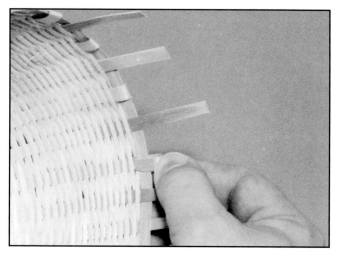

Carriers would have been used by the Shakers for many purposes — from carrying baked goods to articles of fancy work. These useful baskets may have even been helpful in toting personal laundry. I have reproduced the mould for this basket in high impact plastic for the general public (for details, see Supplier List).

The basket shown here is 6″ by 9″ and is 5″ high to the top of the rim. Locate and mark the four corners and the center of this basket, so your weaving will be symmetrical. Draw a grid or pattern as before. Using this bottom pattern, weave so that you do not exceed the limits of the mould. Once you make the bottom of any moulded basket to your satisfaction, make notes about the dimensions of the splint (these will be the same each time, so the materials can be pre-cut).

This carrier is made with a "closed bottom," sometimes called "laid tight." This means that the basket will have no spaces between the bottom weavers. The technique is useful in many baskets, as an alternate bottom construction.

It is essential to weave this bottom with material that is as dry as possible to handle without breaking. Otherwise you must allow the woven bottom to dry before proceeding with the sides, so the splint can shrink to its minimum size. Once you get the formula correct, you can weave several bottoms at a time, let them dry, and then proceed at your convenience.

Using the formula to determine the lengths needed for the uprights (sum of bottom, two side heights, and 1″ allowance for folding over rim), cut them into ½″ widths (remember that the basket is 6″ by 9″ by 5″). "Filler strips" are woven into the basket to eliminate holes in the bottom. This basket will have 9 long uprights and 13 side uprights, giving odd numbers in both directions, which allows for various handle treatments.

Center one short or side upright in the middle of the grid and then place a lengthwise upright over the top and in the middle of the pattern.

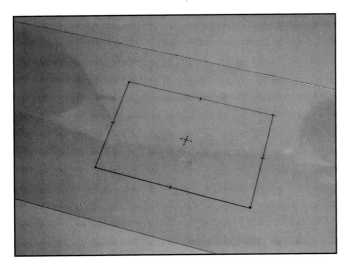

Next use the extra long fillers underneath the side uprights and parallel to the lengthwise upright and close up any spaces.

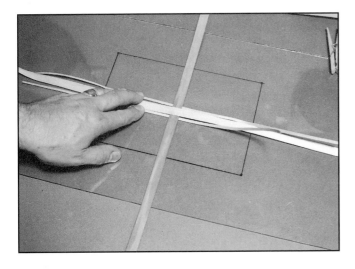

Now weave in side uprights to the left and right of center. If you are doing this correctly, you will notice that the "fillers" are holding the bottom together; if these fillers were removed, the bottom would collapse. Close up the weaving as tightly as possible.

Continue to add, in sequence, building out from the center. Continue to check your spaces and see that you are progressing proportionally so that everything will be used and the bottom will fit within the pattern. Your pattern should look like the one in the photograph below.

Occasional use of a stick as a weaver's beater bar will help tighten up the spaces. Until you get the pattern and process reasonably clear, it is best to build from the center so as to fit the bottom onto the mould and have your uprights nearly even on the edges. In time you may wish to experiment with other techniques that you discover.

Continue to add ribs and fillers until all are used and fill the allotted space. Once the entire grid is filled let it dry completely. The lengthwise uprights should all pass over the two final side uprights added at either end. If they are not symmetrically distant from the center and do not match at each end, locate the center with an X and check your pattern. If you have built with the correct number (uneven) out from the middle, it will match the picture. The long fillers can then be bent back after being dampened and cut to allow them to be tucked under a rib. This secures the last side ribs in place.

Point the ends of the filler strips and tuck them back over themselves toward the center and underneath the closest upright. Some variations in pattern can be achieved depending on where you tuck the ends and how you fill the bottom.

Leave the two fillers nearest the center (marked with an X for clarity) incomplete toward the ends; this is where you will bolt the basket to the mould after adding the keeper strip. For a basket of this size, two fasteners are enough to eliminate any movement on the mould.

Once all the uprights are woven in, check to be sure that you haven't exceeded the corners. Try to stay slightly inside of the bottom pattern to allow for the addition of a "keeper." Starting halfway over the top of an upright and near the midpoint of one side, weave in this fine (1/16″ or less) locking strip to prevent the bottom from shifting. At the corners, fold the keeper to form it neatly; this folded or mitered

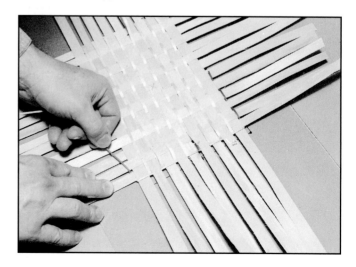

corner is only done with the keeper. I've used a colored keeper here to clearly illustrate this step.

Continue to weave in the keeper, making sure the corners are neatly formed. Once you return to the starting point, overlap the two ends for a distance of four ribs and conceal the joint under a rib.

This process is the same procedure that we used in creating rectangular and square basket bottoms. The use of a keeper prevents bases from shifting as you begin to weave the basket. This procedure also allows you to make basket bases ahead of time and holds their shape while in storage.

Locate the corners onto the mould and drill a hole in the area of the unsecured filler. Add the fasteners and drill the other end and secure.

Trim the extra lengths off the uprights so that the ribs do not surpass the top. Should you wish to later weave a higher basket, weave tight to the mould and allow the longer planned uprights to flare out onto your weaving surface. Remove the basket when nearing the top, as the collar will alter the shape should you weave too far up on the mould, and continue to weave freehand.

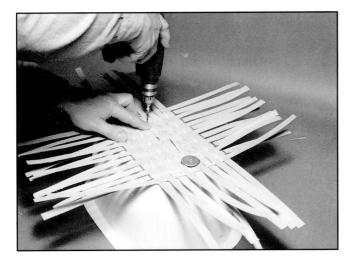

Using scissors, shape the corners so as to allow the uprights to better fill the corners. Make sure your splint is damp to prevent cracking.

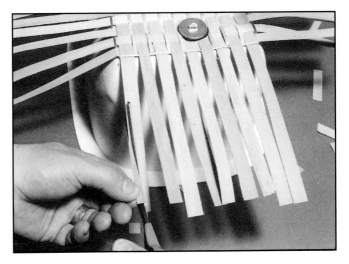

The photograph below shows the shaping and how it will create a better corner appearance. Certain moulds may require shaping of the uprights.

The basket shown in the next photograph will be woven in the more traditional fashion for larger sizes. A split upright located away from the corner and clear of any handle placement will allow us to spiral this basket up.

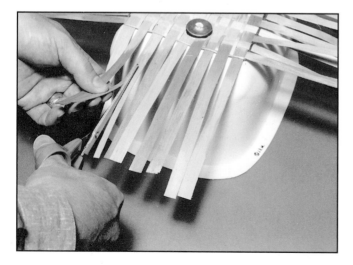

Using a pointed and tapered weaver about ¼″ in width, moisten the uprights and begin to weave with the dampened weaver. Take note of the weaving pattern created by the keeper and start at the split upright. Insert and secure the weaver in the keeper and weave as you would normally. This simple over-under pattern utilizes the split upright as two separate members.

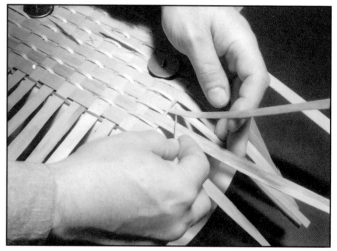

Form the corners and spread the uprights to space them evenly; do not twist or crush the corners. The splints for this basket should be heavier than those used in the previous baskets, simply because of its larger size and the heavier contents it is likely to carry.

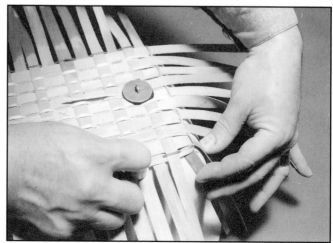

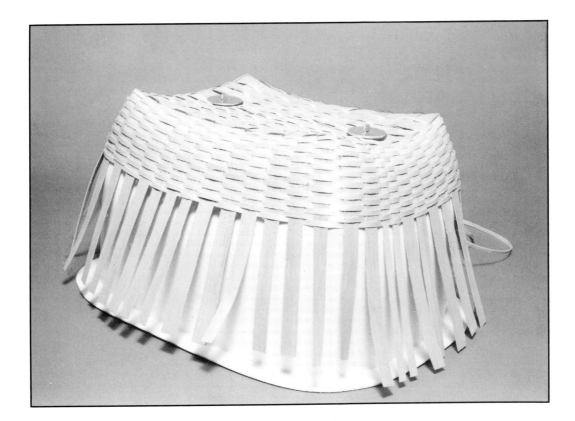

The half-finished basket in the photograph above shows how quickly the form is reached when using the mould, and how uniform it will look.

Once you finish weaving to the desired height, stop the weaver at the split upright and taper the end. The addition of a false rim allows the lashing and the inner and outer rims to be secured to this band and eliminates having to lash into the weavers, which throws off the level of the basket. Remove the basket and begin weaving in a strip of splint the width of the anticipated rim (often the same width as the uprights). Start with the false rim halfway over the top of an upright and weave it in taking note of the weaving pattern below. At the area where you ended your weaving you are going to alter the false rim so as to "lock" in as much of the weaving as possible. The loose tapered ends of the ending weaver can be simply caught in the final lashing process, thereby securing it.

In ending the false rim, float over the beginning point and weave over the top of the lower false rim for a distance of four uprights; cut and secure the end behind the fourth rib. Blunt point or point the ends of the ribs that stick up beyond the false rim and soak them to make them pliable by setting the basket upside down in a shallow pan of water. Do not resoak the whole basket.

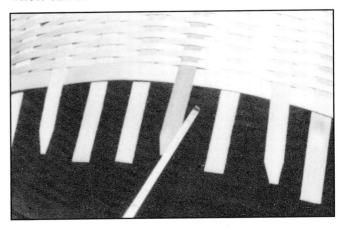

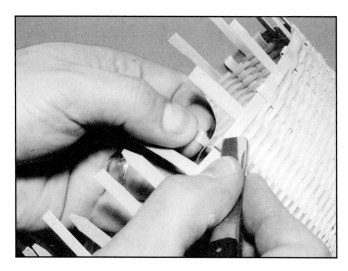

Score any ribs that are too thick to fold over easily with a shallow cut and peel back the excess. Fold the ends of the pointed ribs over the false rim and secure them into the weaving. An awl or other tool will help you open the spaces for the tucked ends.

The final step is to reweave the unsecured fillers to duplicate the others, after moistening them to prevent their breaking off. You are now ready for handles and rims.

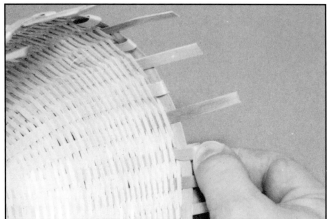

Preparation of rim and handle stock.

I frequently choose hickory for my own basket production as well as for teaching basketry, because it is extremely strong and it resists breaking when used fresh. To further prevent breaking, it can be soaked in water containing fabric softener. However, the wood can become supersaturated and shrinkage must then be considered.

Reed, which can be substituted for rims and handles, frequently returns to its original flat state and often distorts a basket. Bent wood usually requires only a moderate adjustment prior to drying and keeps its shape. I prefer hickory and especially the shag bark (*Carya ovata*) variety for handles and rims, but other hardwoods such as white ash, pig nut hickory, and white oak (*Quercus alba*) can be used as well.

When choosing a hickory tree, select one that is 7″ to 10″ in diameter and has no blemishes. Cut the logs in lengths that correspond to the lengths of your planned baskets' rims (I frequently use 6′ logs to accomplish this purpose).

Once the tree is cut, you can remove the bark from the log and proceed to quarter the tree. The inner bark (closest to the tree) provides splint of a great quality; when peeled carefully, splint seats can be made

from this material. The trees are easily and more accurately quartered if split from the top toward the bottom. It is even easier if the tree is frozen. The split is started in larger logs with a wedge and sledge hammer; finer splitting is started with a froe and mallet. This is accomplished by twisting the froe from side to side so that the split can't travel down the wood. Refer to the diagram to see the pattern or sequence used to split out wood. Once the tree is quartered, that quarter is split in half (#3). The darker heartwood is then removed from the lighter sapwood (#4). Further subdivisions are then made by halving pieces until desired "rough" lengths and widths are achieved (#5 and #6).

At this point your stock is ready to be halved further, either to the growth ring or to the grain depending on the need. If you left the bark on, the hickory bark may be so tough that it throws off splitting. In this case, remove the bark by cutting it away from the wood with a drawknife. Continue to split the wood into smaller more usable "rough" pieces. Remove excess waste or

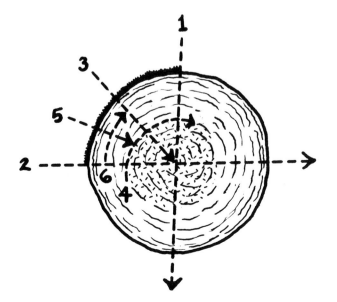

unevenness on the wood in order to split the pieces evenly, but if the pieces are near the size you need leave them alone and use your drawknife.

With a froe, you strike the back of the blade with a mallet to begin the split in the wood. If the split begins to travel off center,

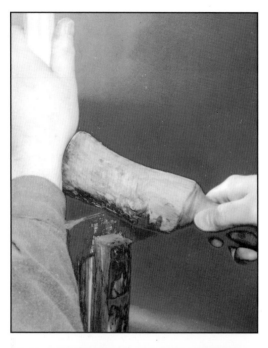

put heavier pressure on the thicker side and ease the split back to the center. Should you have difficulty holding the wood and pulling it apart, place the end in a vise or stand on it. For the finest splitting, you must hold the heels of your palms and your wrists against the outer edges of the wood so that the split travels very slowly. Do it without thought or too fast and you will have kindling! This fine splitting can be started by using a good knife and twisting the blade to start the crack.

A good second choice for handles and rims is the more common white ash (*Fraxinus americana*), which grows at altitudes up to 2,000 feet in the north and 5,000 feet in the south. It has an extensive range and is found in moist well-drained areas populated by other hardwoods. Splint can be pounded off the white ash log and, while harder to work with, provides a resource more common than black ash.

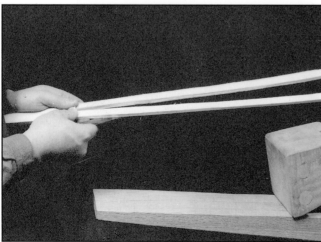

Carving and inserting the cat head handle.

It is always difficult to decide on the proper height of a handle. From years of experience, I have arrived at two formulas that work without fail, both of which are based on proportional considerations of the basket. As usual there is one exception to this rule: handles that are purposely high for a specific reason or function.

The first method uses a tape measure. Start at the top of the rim on one side and measure through the middle of the bottom and back to the top of the rim on the opposite side. On a basket with a diameter of nearly 8″, this length measures 13½″. It must be noted that the measurement is for the handle itself; extra length will be required in order to insert the handle on both ends.

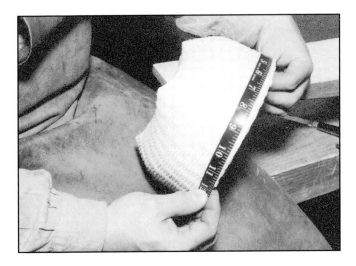

The extra lengths allowed for insertion of the handle are usually more than half the depth of the basket on each side. It is better to cut and taper a longer inserting end than a shorter one. The basket shown here is 5″ high and will need at least 3½″ to 4″ on either end for handle insertion.

Find a piece of fresh or soaked hickory that approaches the required length. The piece shown here is slightly uneven and needs to be sized to a better and more even appearance. It has been split along the intersection of heartwood and sapwood, making a line of demarcation that is a good

The second method is based on a measurement that is one half of the circumference of the basket. To this amount add the two inserting areas. On the same basket as above, this measurement is 12″ without the extra length allowed for handle insertion. As you can see, the difference in these methods is slight.

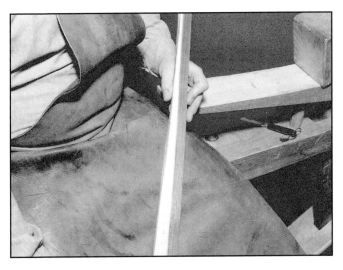

reference point and greatly facilitates splitting. Most wood is less obviously marked, so carefully size your wood to make it even and uniform, thereby reducing the need for guesswork.

The sapwood edge (lighter) is uneven and is heavier at one end; this is where to begin removing the extra wood with a drawknife and shavehorse. I frequently use the curved side of the drawknife blade against the wood; this allows me better control and eliminates fewer abrupt cuts. If you don't have a drawknife and shavehorse, improvise. I have seen students use wood vises, C-clamps, and sawhorses, and other "make-dos." Spokeshaves and a variety of shapers can be substituted and are available at most hardware stores. The tools you require are also available as antiques or reproductions, so shop around.

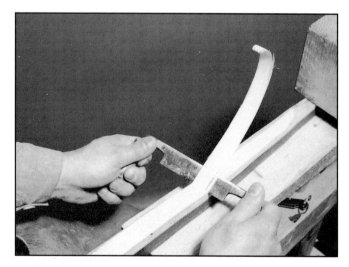

Once the wood is even, it can readily be divided for the cat head basket. A note about the grain of the wood and growth ring pattern will be helpful here. (If you are using reed or one of the varieties of prepared handles, you can disregard this.) Because the wood has been split showing the sapwood line, you can easily see which is the outside (lighter) part. Remember that the growth rings mimic the outer curve of the tree. The convex surface is always the

top or outside of the handle; the inner surface or the area where the rings are concave is where to carve. If you saw the wood, be careful that you don't confuse saw cuts that can resemble growth rings. Wetting the wood will clearly highlight the growth pattern.

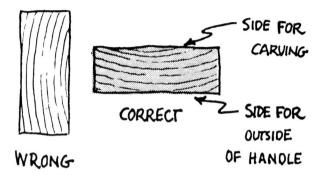

If your billet or stick is slightly oversized, one half of it can be used for the handle and, if long enough, the other half can be re-halved and used for the two rims. Insert a sharp knife between the growth rings and in the middle of the billet; twist it to start a crack.

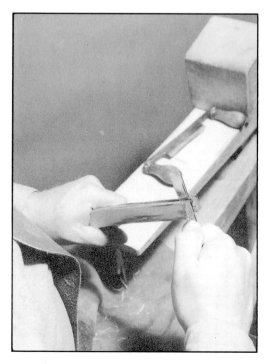

In the photograph below, you can see that the split has started to go off center and so I am exerting extra pressure on the heavier side, "nursing" along the crack on the thinner side until it comes back to center. This process must be done slowly so the stick doesn't break.

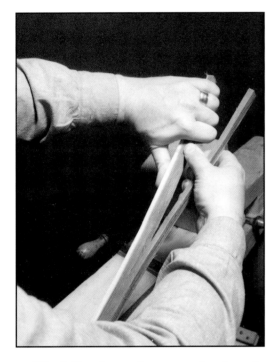

The billet shown here is wider than the handle width needed, so now comes the real test. The grain of the wood runs up and down in this billet. Look to see if splitting the stick in half along the grain (perpendicular/across the growth rings) will give you what you require. Use a drawknife to remove any excess, always carving just halfway and then reversing the cut. Because this billet is large enough, a knife blade can be inserted halfway and twisted to open the crack. The knife is used as a mini-froe, to coax the crack down the piece of wood.

The resulting piece of wood is slightly less than ½"; the final carving will bring it down to the width of the upright against which it will be inserted. If the handle is narrower than the rib or upright, it will be loose and may rock back and forth in the basket.

Place the sapwood side (convex side) against the shavehorse and mark out the handle onto the heartwood surface (concave). Mark the total handle length, includ-

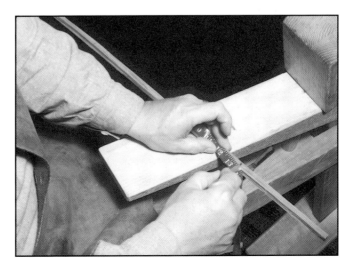

ing allowance for insertion, equidistant from both ends of the billet. Now mark the insertions with a soft lead pencil.

Using a drawknife, begin to carve the handle slightly off the insertion mark and toward the center, perhaps ¼″ to create a lug or shoulder. Carve only halfway and reverse the stock in the jaw of the shavehorse. Repeat the lug formation step and carve again toward the center. Do this slowly, taking away small amounts at a time so you can see what you are doing. A full-length cut will remove the lug area you are creating on the opposite end. Continue to remove the handle to check progress.

control your carving by holding your knife still and pulling the wood into the blade by sliding it on leather.

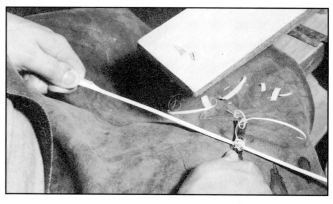

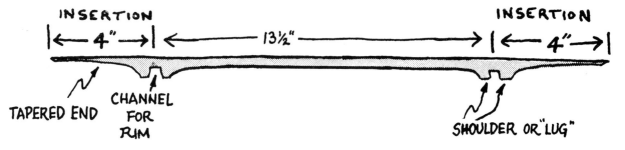

INSERTION
|← 4″ →| ← 13½″ → | |← 4″ →|

TAPERED END   CHANNEL FOR RIM   INSERTION   SHOULDER OR "LUG"

Mark a ¾″ shoulder or lug area where the rim will be placed. Taper the remaining ends in a sloping fashion so that the tips are extremely thin and can be easily inserted into the basket. Chamfer or bevel the edges to remove their harsh 90° angles and smooth by scraping or sanding. It is easy to

Point or blunt point just the tips of the inserting ends; don't narrow the width as this keeps the handle from rocking.

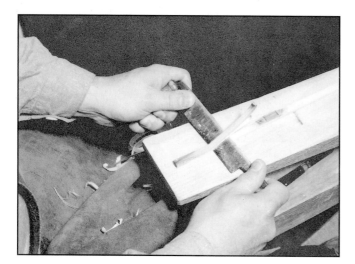

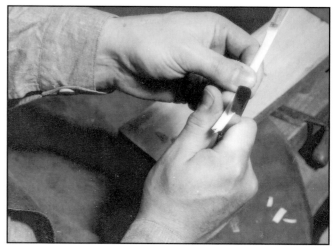

Carefully flex the handle and bend it into the anticipated shape. Check it to see how it looks in the basket and if it needs any other details or refinement. Skip a number of weavers and insert the tab down against a center rib (use a cut rib if available). Insert the other tab into the opposite rib. Check to see if the handle is centered (it is easier than you think to place it incorrectly). You may leave the handle in this position while preparing the rims.

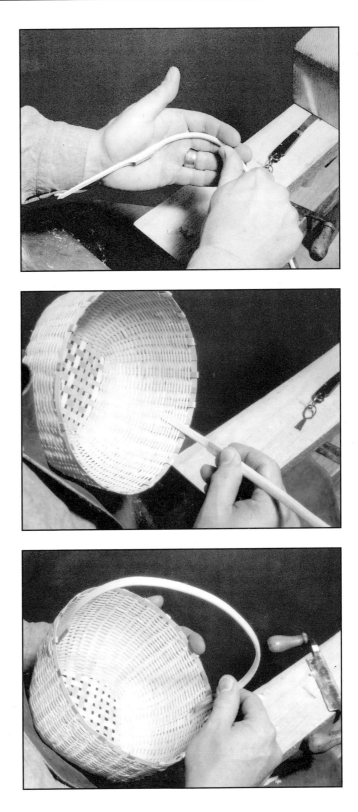

Carving the spoon basket handles.

The type of small handles for the spoon basket, shown below, are frequently carved and used as "steeples" or "ears" on which a swing handle pivots. Larger versions of this handle with a bigger opening between the lugs gives another shape for use on field or other baskets. The two handles are carved as one, then split apart and finished.

On the concave ring surface, mark an inch on either side of the center. This handle will only be 2″ from lug to lug, so delicate work is necessary to make this handle appear correct.

With the curved side of the drawknife down, start to cut away the waste toward the center. Reverse this process and remove the waste. Continue to carve this miniature handle until a delicate well-profiled shape is achieved.

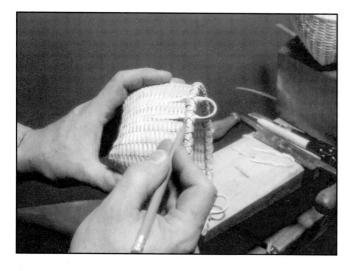

Take a piece of hickory 6-7″ long and 1″ wide and approximately ¾″ thick. The measurements are all larger than the finished size, providing some extra materials in case of a complication. Place the hickory with the convex growth rings to the outside of the handle (against the shaving surface).

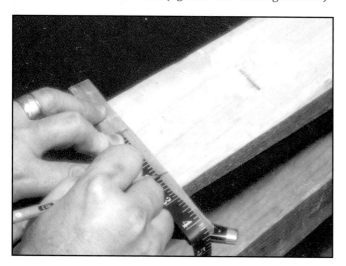

If the stock has been prepared correctly and the grain is straight, you can now split across the growth ring and form two handles. If you are successful on the first try, you can resplit the halves as they will be too large at this point. If the split ran off center, you probably have plenty to carve away with the drawknife to end up with two handles.

The handles should look like those in the photograph below. Further carving and chamfering is done at this time, as a chamfered edge helps the handle bend better. Carefully bend the handle to see how it performs and looks.

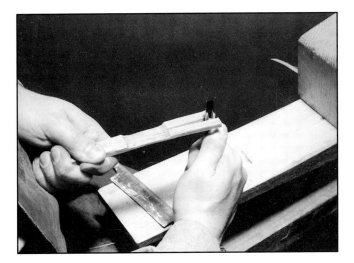

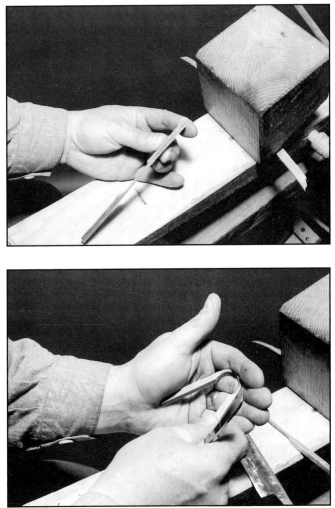

Straighten it out and reinsert it into the jaw of the shavehorse, rotating it 45° from its original position. Carve this surface with the growth rings on end to produce a delicate shoulder to receive the rim. This lug or shoulder area is no more than ½″ —less is better than more in Shaker baskets. If you are confused, study the photograph.

The photograph below shows the finished and inserted handle. Notice that the marker created notches to show you where the rims will be placed.

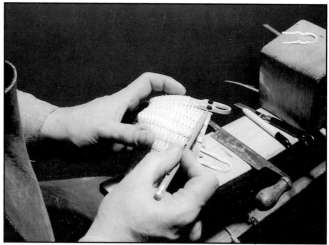

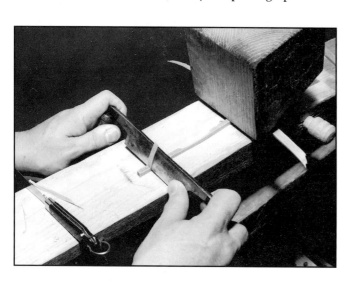

Carving the personal carrier handles.

Using different handles on this basic form will alter the look and function of this basket. The Shakers wove various heights of baskets on a single mould and varied the handles to create different looks and uses.

The photograph below shows larger versions of the handles created for the spoon basket. The positioning shows that three uprights were used to keep the ribs even on either side of the handle. An uneven number (9, in this case) was needed to keep the handle centered.

The photograph below shows another possibility for inserting a handle lengthwise; obviously, extra length had to be allowed in carving. This handle is the same style as the cat head handle. It has a channel cut in the lug or shoulder area to receive the rim. This notch is marked for clarity in the photograph.

The simple notched handle in the photograph below is calculated using our previous formulas for length. The lug area is an easily carved notch that will prevent the handle from being removed once the rim is lashed in place.

The photograph below shows the difference between these two styles. The more complex channel notched handle is more common in Shaker work. However, the basket that is reproduced here has the easier handle, as well as a single heavy rim on the inside and a dress splint lashed to the outside. The dress splint conceals both the false rim and the construction aspects. Most Shaker work uses two matched rims, but this technique was used on occasion.

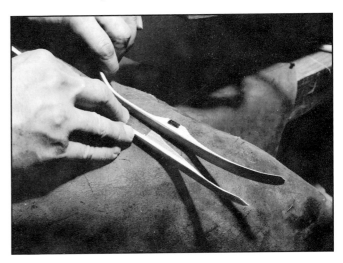

Carving the rims.

To judge the lengths of wood needed for the rims, measure the outside circumference of the basket top. You can also multiply the diameter times Pi (3.14) to get the circumference. Add to that measurement a minimum of 3″ for overlaps and you have the length of stock necessary. The basket shown is 7½″ in diameter. By multiplying 7.5 x 3.14 and then adding 3″ for overlap, the result is a 27″ length cut for the rim. If you can't remember all this math, simply measure the outer circumference and give yourself a good overlap.

The wood is then halved to the size that is nearly required; this final division halves the stock along the growth rings. The rings will be parallel to the side of the basket and will curve toward the outside.

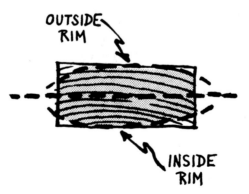

OUTSIDE RIM

INSIDE RIM

Insert a knife blade along the center growth ring and urge the crack evenly along the length of the stock. Control the pull by exerting inward pressure with your wrists to prevent the crack from travelling too fast.

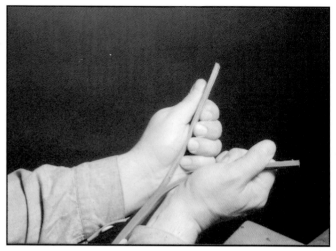

Carve the rims, working halfway at a time and then reversing direction. Because the rims are flat ovals without any special lugs or shoulders, you may occasionally work in both directions — toward center and away from center. Remember, hold your blade stationary and pull the wood into the blade.

This distinctive variation allows you to be able to carve even rims, but it must be done with care. The look of the cross section should be a flat oval or half round. The thickness of these carved rims will be about 1/8″; anything heavier would overpower this basket. (If you use commercial half round reed, you might want to carve it down.) Remember that the rims are held apart by the basket; this additional thickness will give flat ovals a round appearance when lashed to the basket.

Insert the carved interior rim, carved concave rings to the outside (see rim diagram), and position the rim in the center of the lug or shoulder area. Mark on either side to indicate width and place a reference mark showing the direction inserted and the location of the fit. The rim width will be as large or slightly larger than the false rim, to conceal this construction.

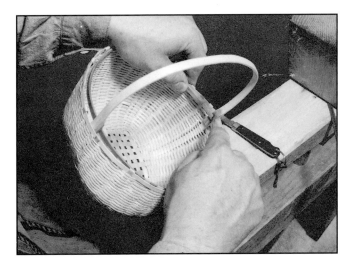

With a saw, make a cut inside your pencil lines. Don't cut right on the lines because the space or channel created will be too large and when the rims shrink, they will be sloppy and the handle will rock from side to side. Fit the rims as tightly as you can. Saw more than halfway into the channel area; too much wood left there and the rim will stand out too far from the

basket and create unsightly gaps. Once the rim is permanently in place, it will support this thin area.

Keep the cuts even in depth. Should they be uneven, when the waste is "popped" out it could split off the lug necessary to hold the rim in place. Insert the knife blade into this cut and using the strongest section of the blade twist the knife until the waste cracks free.

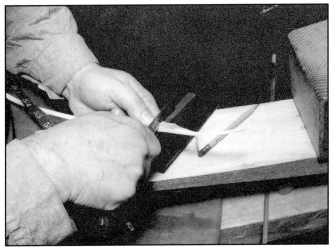

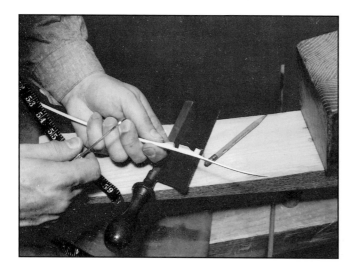

With the shavehorse, gradually take off the extra on either end. Do not start with a quick cut — anything but a gradual taper with nearly nothing taken off the beginning will spell a disaster at worst or a poor fit at best. Round the covering end and refit the rim to the inside of the basket. Moisten to prevent it from sliding around. Clamp the ends with a spring clamp or clothespins.

Position the rims and check the fit. Lightly mark the overlaps with a soft pencil. The overlaps can be near the handle but preferably not right at the handle, for strength considerations. Carefully taper or scarf the overlapped ends until the two ends together are the same thickness as a single thickness of the rim.

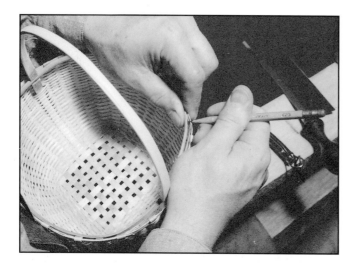

Repeat this process for the outside rim. Once you have finished, make some notes; this will be a standard size you can use. (The Shakers sometimes pre-formed these pieces and put the basket together in what we might call assembly line fashion.) Place the overlaps of the outside rim near the overlaps that are on the inside. This positioning will allow you to tighten the basket completely when you do the lashing. Clamp the outside rim in place and prepare lashing splints.

The same process is used for all other rim styles. Single rims may take less time, but are not always used by the Shakers. Aesthetic judgment will affect your choice of rim treatments and handles, just as it did with the Shakers, but quality should never be sacrificed.

While the Shakers cross
bound or double lashed baskets for strength
or aesthetic consideration, other lashing
variations were also used. To lash with just
one piece, use six times the basket circumference as a measurement guide. The lasher
is what holds everything together, so don't
use too narrow a piece; the lashing strip
shown here is ¼″ wide.

Start to the right of the outside overlap
(if you are right-handed) and insert the wet
lashing strip under the rim and the interior
false rim strip.

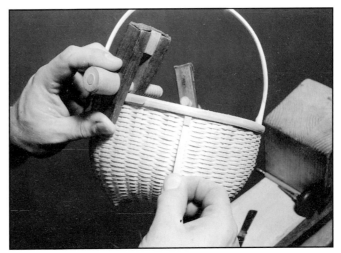

Now begin to lash over the top of both
rims, bringing the end of the lasher (now
pointed) through each hole or space between the uprights. You will be lashing to
the right at this time. Be careful to pull
tightly on the lasher. Remember to lash just
below the false rim — do not pull any
weavers into this process. Lash only the
two tapered ends which are left floating
from the weaving.

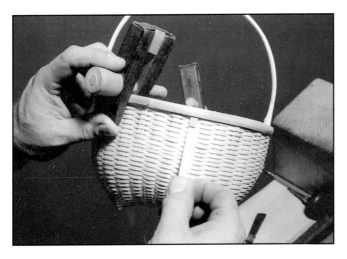

Loop it over the top of the false rim and
push it between the false rim and the actual
outside rim; pull this loop down until it is
taut and secure.

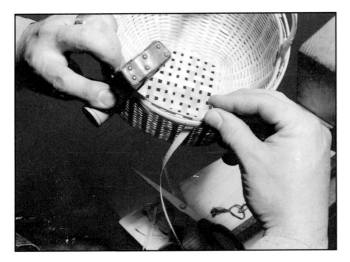

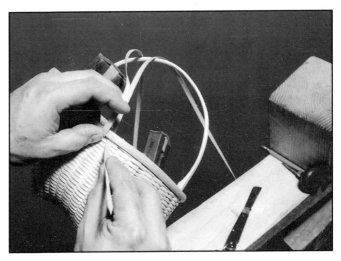

Cross over at the handle and continue to lash as before. If you wish to lash only in one direction, cross the handle now (refer to lashing diagram A). Continue to lash until all the spaces are used. When the single lashing is complete, bring the end up between the inner rim and the false rim. Then take the end over the top of the false rim and in between the outside rim and cut off.

If cross lashing (binding) is desired, a simple reversing of the lasher and heading backwards (to the left) is all that is required. If the slight gap at this point bothers you, an alternate method can be used: come up from the inside with the lasher underneath the inside rim and in between the rim and the false rim. Loop the lasher over the top of the false rim and pull it down securely between the false rim and the outside rim. This technique is identical to ending single lashing, but you do not cut off the lasher. You have now reversed the direction of the lasher, heading to the left through the same spaces as before. Cross over the handles to create the X on the outside; in between the handles, form the X on top of the rims.

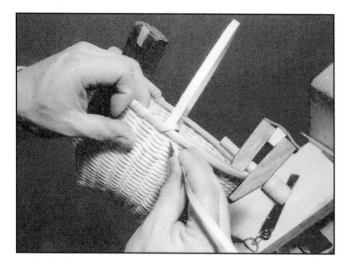

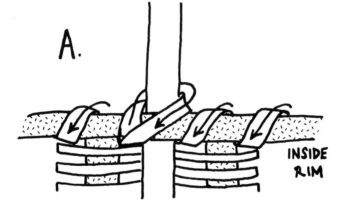

A.

INSIDE RIM

B.

To end, come up under the inner rim on the last pass and pull tight. Be sure your lashing strip is not too dry. Open a space between the false and the outer rims and to the left where the lasher can be pulled down and secured. Clip the remaining end.

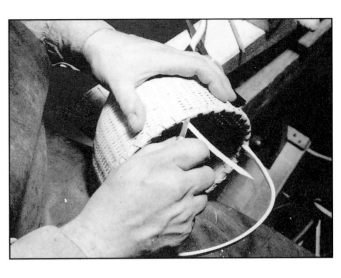

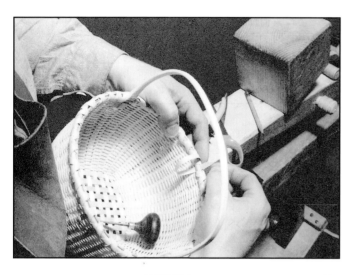

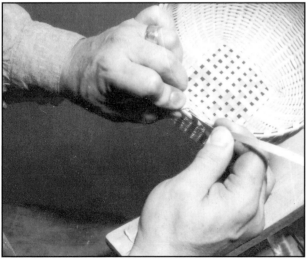

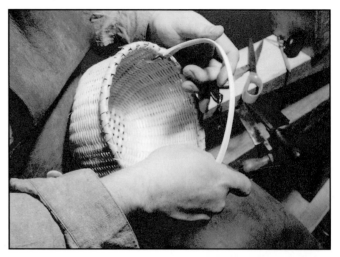

After lashing, shape the basket and handles so that they can dry in the proper form. A squaring of the handle completes the cat head basket. The classic squared handle is frequently referred to as a "bonnet handle" as it resembles the squared brim of a Shaker Sister's bonnet.

One final note: should you run out of lasher and have to join in another strip, end as you would normally. Take a second strip and secure it either from the inside or outside depending on what direction your lashing is headed. If you are in a hurry, a simple tuck up and under the rims is usually enough to secure a start.

Congratulations! You have finished lashing your basket(s) and have learned a number of techniques that will be useful for any basket that you make, Shaker or other.

If you decide to add cleats (skids) into the bottom of a basket, thin down the ends of heavier splints or hickory and catch them into the bottom while still wet and flexible. (see photograph at right) Or you can lash, rivet, or nail larger pieces of wood called "skates" onto the basket. Skates were often found on wood chip baskets and made it easy to pull the baskets along icy paths. The photograph at lower right shows shaped skids which have been inserted in the pattern to allow the basket bottom to "wear" better. This finishing detail can be used in round baskets of a single or double bottom construction.

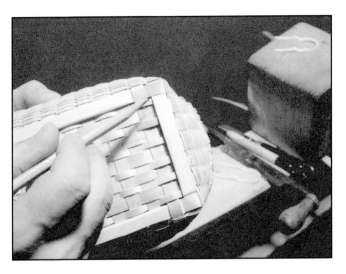

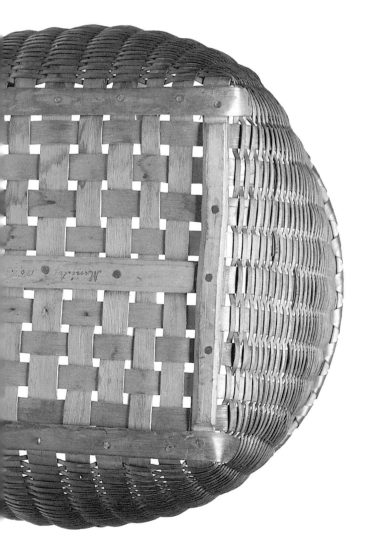

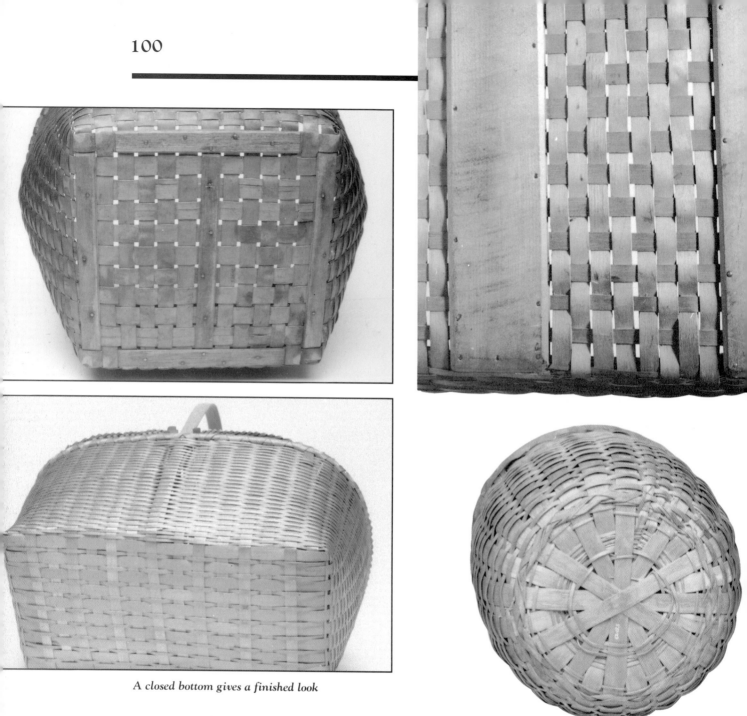

A closed bottom gives a finished look

An extra lashed on cross bound skid

. Most details are added after the basket is finished, which makes possible the continual replacement of these "add on" parts. The photographs here show this and other finishing aspects — study them carefully and be creative! Careful attention to all details give a more finished look.

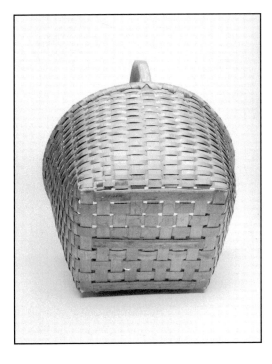

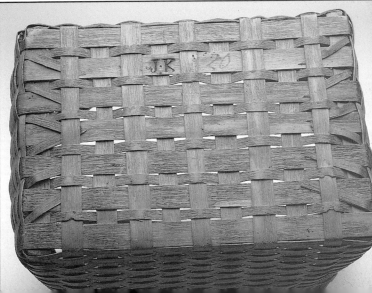

Making a pin cushion basket.

The materials used for this basket and a variation of this form using a handle and matching rims of a contrasting wood create a different look and function. Using this same method, the Shakers created different baskets from the same moulds.

Start by making a pattern on the bottom of a piece of plexiglass. If using a water soluble pen turn over the pattern so as to protect the pattern from getting wet.

Because there is an even number of dampened uprights (8 in both directions), do not start directly in the middle of the pattern. Start with three horizontal ribs that are parallel to each other and weave in three

verticals. This will lock the grid and allow you to weave outward. Keep adjusting the holes or open spaces as you proceed and note that you are not filling the pattern irregularly. When making a very small basket, keep the holes in the bottom very close together.

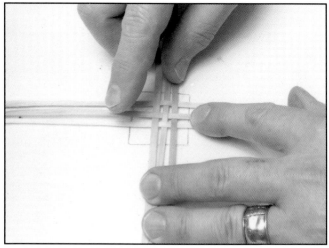

Do not let the size of the bottom exceed the pattern you have drawn. Add the keeper strip around the bottom, as in the previous baskets. Secure the damp bottom onto the mould with tacks or pushpins.

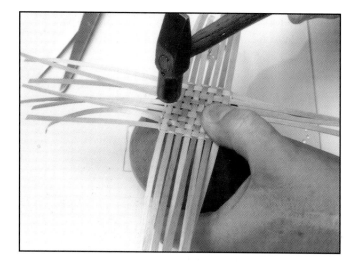

At a corner, begin in the middle of the thread-like center and weave in the splint opposing the pattern of the keeper. Form the corners carefully.

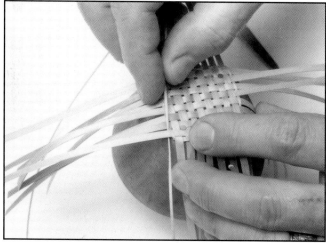

The sides will be woven with the chase weaving technique, as in previous baskets. Starting as in all chase weaving projects, cut an elongated hourglass shape away from the middle of the starting weaver and for this project a distance of 2 inches. This shaping should take the center of the weaver to a thread-like fineness. The weaver shown here is already cleaned on both sides to a paper thinness and is cut to an even 1/16″ width. Remember not to do this shaping directly in the middle as we wish to stagger the joining of additional weavers.

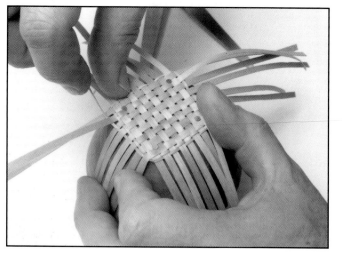

Once you return to the starting point, fold over the remaining half of the weaver and weave it into the basket heading in the same direction as before. You will now have two weavers headed in the same direction and staggered behind each other; they will be treated as separate weavers throughout the basket.

To splice new weavers: end the old weaver over the top of an upright and thin the end if desired; count back four uprights and secure the new weaver under that upright; weave over the top of the bottom weaver (your weaving will be doubled up) until you cover the stop and continue weaving.

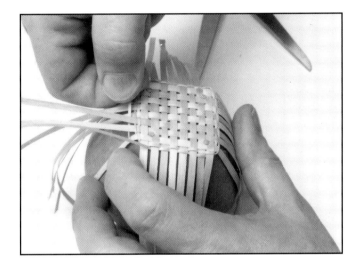

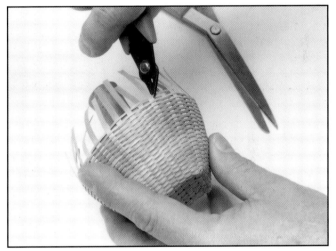

Continue to form the corners and begin to fan out the uprights to create an even distance between them. This will produce the uniform shape and spacing so characteristic of Shaker workmanship. Keep the weaving tight to the previous row and keep the ribs close to the mould by pressing them to the form as you weave over them.

The photograph above shows that we have woven up to the top of the basket, to the desired height. Stop on the same corner and just slightly stagger the weavers behind adjacent uprights; ending the weavers this close to each other and behind uprights has some benefits, especially when the weavers are this narrow. It allows the false rim to be woven in without altering the pattern, as in the cat head basket.

Unweave the weavers and taper the ends to a point. Reweave them so that the points will tuck behind the adjacent ribs (in this basket they should be right next to each other). It is possible to stagger them further apart but with such fine material it is unnecessary.

Weave in a band of wide splint the width of the rim you anticipate and about the same thickness as your uprights. Frequently the rim will be the same width as the widest upright. Starting over the top of an upright and in any position, weave in this band contrary to the pattern below.

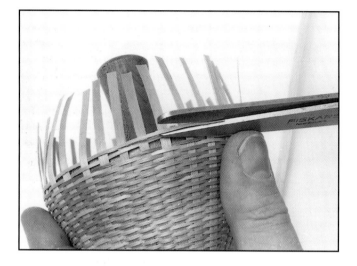

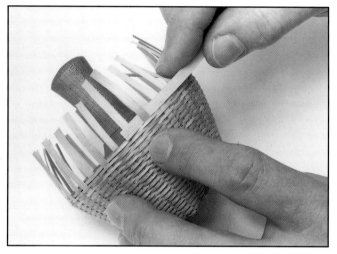

The photograph below shows how the false rim is doubled up for a distance of four uprights and the end is concealed behind a spoke. The weight of splint in fine baskets is very important; the weavers should not overpower the uprights.

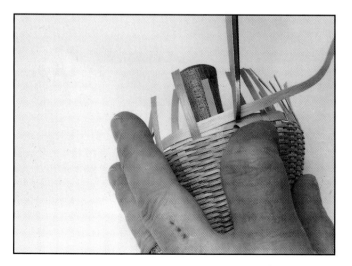

Pry the tacks or pushpins loose and remove the basket from the mould. Let the basket dry for at least a full day. When dry, pack down the weavers to eliminate looseness.

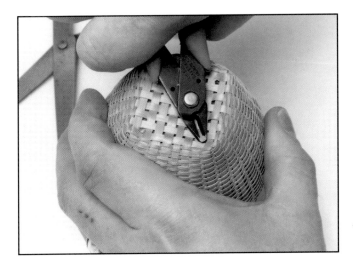

On the outside of the basket place an additional covering strip of splint the width of the piece used at the top. You can secure the beginning behind an upright to eliminate unnecessary clamps to hold it.

Lap this covering piece over itself a distance of a few spokes and cut it off. This covering piece will help stabilize the lashing.

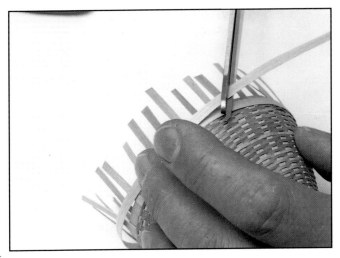

Use a very thin, wet, and cleaned lasher the width of the distance between the spokes and a minimum of three times the circumference in length. Secure the beginning behind the covering piece and leave a tab which you will cut later.

Fold over the lasher and lash from left to right. This procedure will allow you to work from the outside to the inside (this is a different method from the normal inside to outside lashing).

The photograph below illustrates the technique of lashing this basket on a diagonal. You can crease the fold for a neater appearance. I suggest you start to the right of the overlap so you can tighten as you proceed.

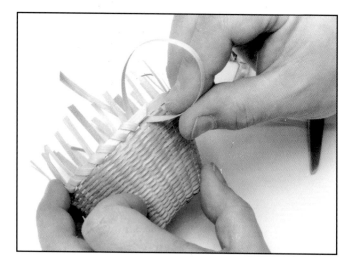

Once you have completed the diagonal lashing around the basket, bring the last overcast underneath the covering piece and pull taut. You may cut this end now, but be aware that it is a very fragile ending and undue stress will cause it to ravel out. To help eliminate this problem, delay cutting it until nearly finished or add an additional inside cover piece at the top (this additional splint will give another piece to help you secure your ends and conceal construction).

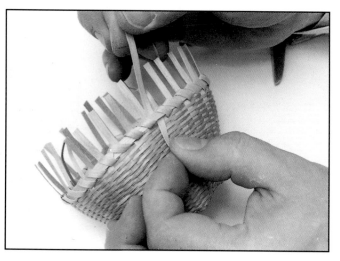

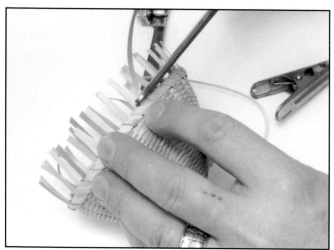

Fold over the dampened thin uprights and on the diagonal pass the ends through the folded edge and pull taut. If you wish, clip off the starting end once you are sure things are secure. The photograph shows how the little floating pointed ends of the weavers are secured; they are very thin and can be caught with the lashing. Continue to fold back the uprights and secure on a diagonal and then clip off the excess ends.

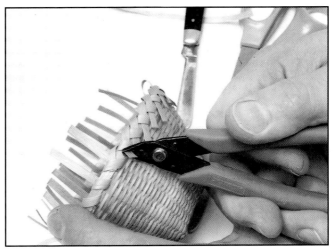

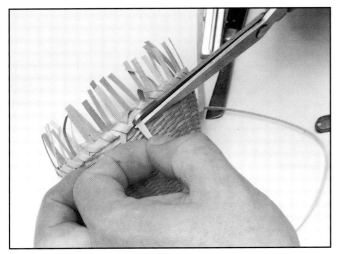

Should you wish to add a handle to this basket as seen in the photo below; make sure you use an uneven number of uprights in both directions to allow for handle placement.

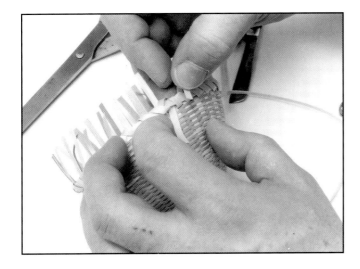

Making an 8 over 8 or double bottom basket.

This basket is sometimes referred to as a demi-john basket because of the hump in the bottom. The hump, which is created during construction, is frequently accentuated so that the weight of the contents is evenly distributed throughout the bottom rather than in the middle. In a few antique photographs the hump is exaggerated to the point where its intent is unclear, however this two-bottom technique creates strength and a pleasing appearance.

The photograph on the opposite page shows this basket in an unfinished state on the mould. The finished basket in the photograph is made with a contrasting manzanita handle which gives this form a new look. The materials in the photograph should give you a feeling of the fineness required in materials; wider and heavier uprights and weavers can change the look and function of the piece.

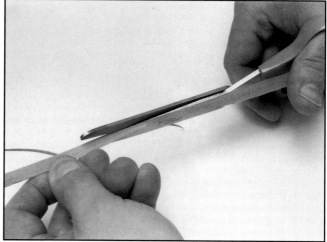

To begin, determine the length of the uprights, adding to the anticipated finished height an inch on each end. Determine the width of the uprights; there will be 16 uprights so they shouldn't be too wide or too narrow. The uprights used here are about ½″ wide and 16″ long.

Once you have cut the length and determined a width that seems suitable, carefully fold the wet uprights or ribs in half so as to determine their center points. With scissors, narrow a four-inch stretch of the middle in a gradual hourglass shape (this can be done by eye or traced by a pattern). The narrower you shape the uprights in the center, the closer in you can start weaving and the quicker you can add the second set of ribs — resulting in the 8 over 8 or double bottom.

The distance between the ribs shown in the photograph below is about the maximum that you would want before using a wider rib. Take note of the best side of the splint; when weaving with a mould, you want the best side facing you.

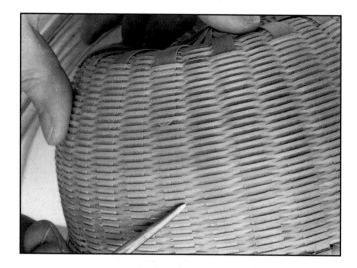

Select four uprights and space them 45° apart as shown in the photograph below. Remember to have the best surface on the top. Add the remaining four uprights in sequential order, dividing the initial pie-shaped spaces into halves.

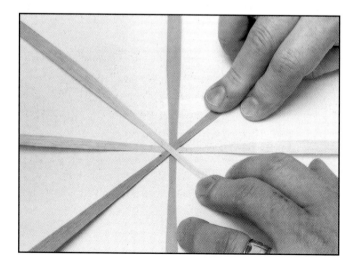

Add the usual keeper strip to lock the uprights in position. Overlap this damp strip of fine weaver a distance of about four ribs, conceal the end behind an upright, and cut away the excess. If you are unsure about this step, refer back to the beginning projects.

This basket uses the chase weaving technique of previous baskets. Cut well-cleaned weavers that are about 20% lighter in thickness than the uprights to 3/32″ in width. This basket, like all of the fancy Shaker baskets, has a delicate appearance due to the fineness of materials.

Making an 8 over 8 or double bottom basket.

Begin with dampened weavers; select out one piece and fold it over away from the center. Cut an elongated hourglass shape, reducing the weaver to a thread-like center. Start in the middle of the thinned weaver and weave as you would any basket. Take note of the pattern caused by the keeper and weave contrary to that row.

When you have woven out from the center to a point where a second set of uprights can be added, place a narrowed upright to check if it can be accommodated into the weaving. If not, weave further out from the center or narrow the uprights more. The photographs below show that I chose to further narrow the uprights as I prefer to add the second set of uprights as quickly as reasonable.

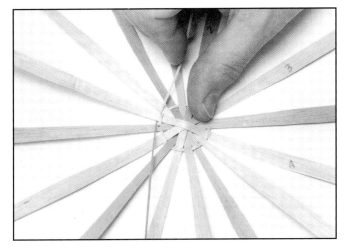

When you come around to the starting point, fold under the remaining portion of the first weaver and weave in the same direction. You will now have two weavers headed in the same direction; this is chase weaving and allows you to weave an even number of uprights in a spiral pattern. You will now treat these two weavers as distinct elements and continue to join and weave two throughout the basket.

The photograph shows that the first of the next set of 8 uprights has been woven in. It is added on the up stroke of the weaving pattern where it can be caught and secured in place. Add the remaining seven of the second set of uprights in a sequence, carefully bisecting the center to keep them in order. The hump that is forming in the middle is created by the materials laying on top of each other and will later be accen-tuated. The photograph shows how the second chasing weaver must be used next or the weaving pattern will be off. Continue weaving with both strands, joining as necessary when the weavers end.

If you prefer, the second set of uprights can be added to the inside of the basket rather than the outside. To do this, turn the bottom over when you have woven out from the center enough to accommodate the second set of uprights. You were weaving clockwise on the outside of the basket and now the weaving direction is reversed. You will only weave "backwards" until the second set of uprights is secured. Flip the bottom back to the outside and continue weaving the base.

Making an 8 over 8 or double bottom basket.

Keep the weavers moist but not wet, as shrinkage will show here. Weave tightly to keep the work uniform. Weave the bottom so that it fits the mould and then secure it to the mould with tacks. From this point, weave up the sides to the top of the mould. The width of the weavers can be graduated during weaving to vary the look of the basket. To accentuate the hump, dampen the bottom and gently flex up the center.

Stagger the ends of the chase weavers so that they are not next to each other; this may be necessary for leveling the appearance of the basket. Let the basket dry completely and then tighten the weaving. Taper back the ends of the weavers; conceal them behind uprights and apart from each other. Their proximity to each other depends on the width of weavers.

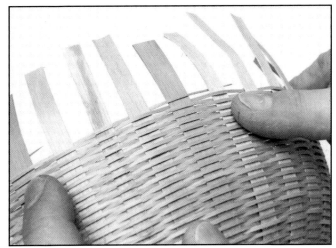

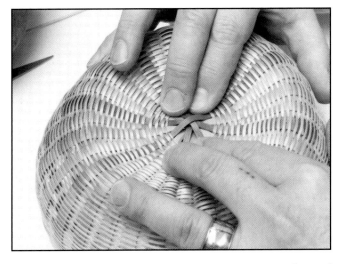

The appearance of this bottom is achieved by adding the second set of uprights to the inside.

Using a dampened heavy splint, add a false rim above the last row of weaving as in previous baskets. Start anywhere and over the top of a rib. Weave in this strip cut to the width of the anticipated rim. Keep the weaving pattern contrary to the weaving below and alter (skip over or under) the pattern if necessary to lock in the weaving. This may be necessary to do twice. Double over the top of the false rim a distance of four uprights and cut the remainder off; secure the end behind an upright.

Wet the tops of the remaining uprights and thin any ribs that appear too thick to easily bend over the false rim. Score them and peel them thinner for ease in manipulation. Blunt point the dampened ends of the uprights that are on the outside of the false rim; fold them over and secure into the weaving. Cut the remaining inside uprights flush with the false rim.

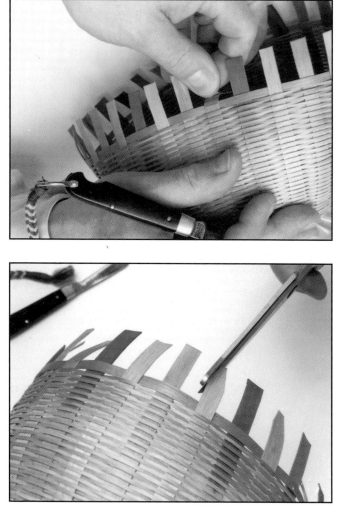

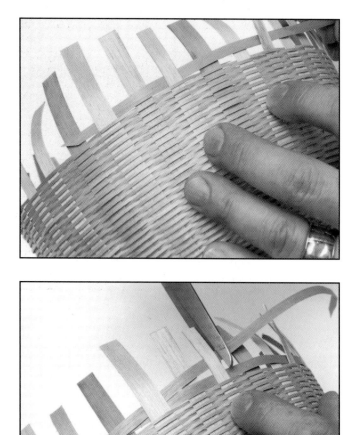

Making an 8 over 8 or double bottom basket.

You can now carve your handle(s) and rims and finish lashing this project. A variety of handle styles such as this heart handle can be used to vary the look/function of your basket. To protect the bottom of the basket and vary its look, skids or runners can be inserted into the weaving, as shown.

Making a fancy rectangular basket with decorative bands.

This basket is made on a wooden mould that you can easily shape at home. Because much of this project is redundant in its weaving, I will eliminate several steps and highlight the parts that make this basket different from others. Refer to the weaving instructions for previous baskets, if necessary.

The photograph on the opposite page shows the basket in its completed state and the forms that are used in its making. The unusual mould with the vertical fasteners is used to shape rims for the basket should you wish to achieve a production mode in creating its elements.

This basket is about 2½″ by 4½″ long and is woven to a height of 2½″. It has 13 side uprights (an uneven number of side uprights is needed so that the handle can be centered) and 8 lengthwise uprights. The ribs or uprights are a flexible and thin 3/16″. If you have trouble making these fancy baskets, it is usually because the material is too heavy. It must be very thin so the materials easily slide on themselves and are not distorted. Weavers should always be less heavy than the uprights but not fragile to the point of being easily distorted.

Weave the base of the basket out from the center and add the keeper strip, as in the cat head basket. Use pushpins or tacks to secure the base onto the mould. If the head of the tack is small, drive the nail through a piece of wood to allow the nail to hold better; this way, the head will not pull through.

Moisten the uprights and fold them down against the mould; pre-form the corners to get the material shaped. Now you are going to add a wide band to begin weaving the basket. This wide weaver helps create a neater corner, especially when used with others to form the starting corners. The Shakers used this technique and used other bands further up in the weaving to create a design element. Start to add this wider weaver off the corner and begin over the top of an upright; you can thin the starting end (and the overlapping finishing end) to prevent a bump in the weaving.

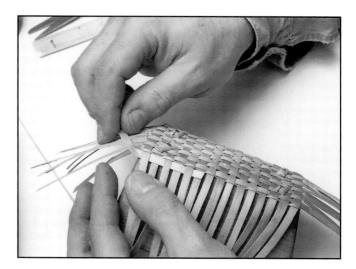

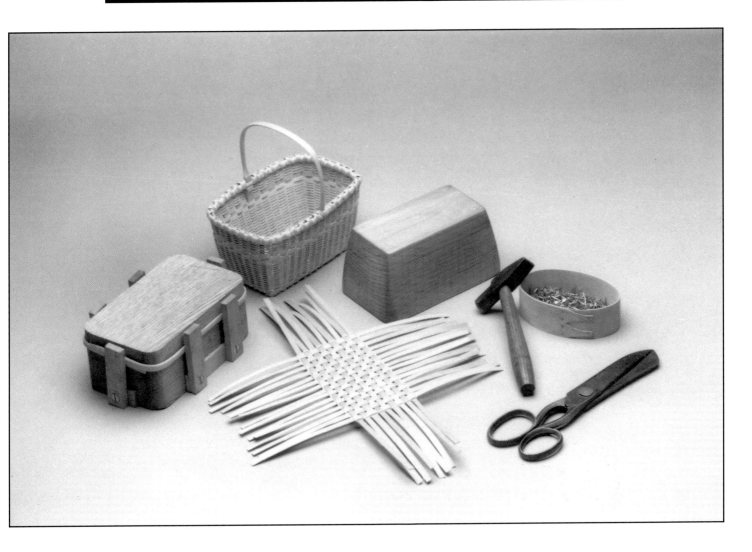

Form each corner neatly and make sure that you are weaving a pattern opposed to the keeper strip below. Overlap the ends of weavers and secure them as shown. If this technique is followed, no loose ends will need to be cut on the basket.

The sides will be woven with the chase weaving technique of previous baskets. Use a weaver that is slightly thinner in weight than the upright and about 1/16" wide. As with all chase weaving, fold the weaver off center and for a distance of 4" cut an elongated hourglass shape so the center of the weaver is thread-like.

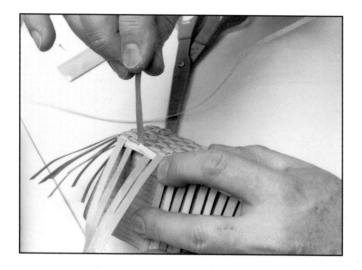

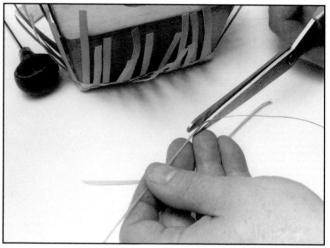

Begin another row of the wide band in a different place so as to vary the starts and add to the look of the work. Tighten and neaten the work as you go.

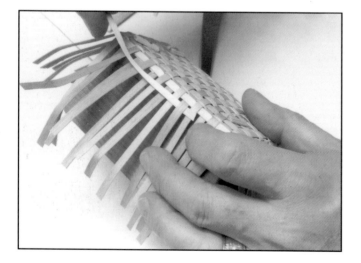

Making a fancy rectangular basket with decorative bands.

Starting at or near the corner and taking note of the opposing weaving pattern below, place the center of the hourglass on the corner and begin to weave. Tighten as you go. Take the other end of the weaver, fold it back on itself and weave it in opposing the pattern below. You are now weaving with two strands headed in the same direction but in opposing patterns. You will now treat these ends as two weavers and join additional weavers on both ends until reaching the desired height. Remember to push the uprights against the mould as you weave over them. It requires only a slight tension on the weavers to make the basket conform to the shape.

The decorative band(s) can be added at any point. Simply stop the weaving of the two chasing weavers at the corner you began. Slightly taper the ends and stagger them next to each other, with the ends behind an upright. The following weaver ends one upright behind the leader. The tapering and stopping in this position will help keep the weaving level. Now weave in a band of the wider weaver in the same fashion as you began the bottom. If you oppose the weaving below, you will lock in the weaving and when you come around to the corner where you stopped weaving the tapered ends can be easily concealed. Add as many bands as you wish. Remember to stagger the starts as with the first two bands at the bottom. Restart the chase weave as before and finish the basket. Don't forget the false rim at the top, as in the previous baskets. Allow the basket time to dry and tighten before finishing the top.

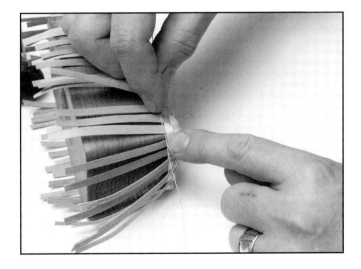

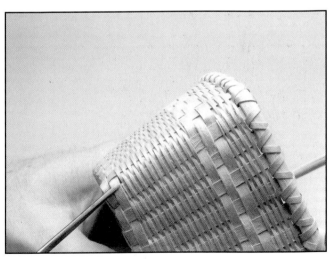

Making a fancy twilled basket lid.

One of the most elegant forms produced by the Shakers was the lidded basket with a twilled design in the lid. The photograph on the opposite page shows a finished basket and various pieces used in the lid construction. The fine cutting gauge is used to produce the uprights and horizontal spokes; slightly finer and thinner weavers are used in the actual weaving. Note that superfine material is used in these more refined pieces; the splint was halved and then rehalved to produce the fineness necessary. *(See splint preparation section for this process and repeat the procedure to achieve the necessary thinness.)* Sanding or scraping may be further employed to achieve the desired results.

In fancy Shaker baskets, such as this one, the material is extremely thin so that you can slide it tight to itself without producing gaps or unsightly distortions. Use longer pieces of splint to begin, so that length is not a concern. Work with slightly dry black ash so that gaps don't result in the work due to excessive shrinkage. It is best to give yourself time to allow the basket to dry and then tighten the weaving between steps.

Start with very thin splint which has been cut to approximately 1/16″ and cleaned on both sides so that there is not a big textural difference. The lid shown here is being done with a small amount of the fibrous cambium remaining on one side of the upright and laterals to highlight some construction aspects. Start by folding them over a semi-circular stick which is in cross section and longer than the width of the anticipated project. In this project, it is begun by folding over eleven pieces of the 1/16″ uprights and securing them with the lateral material of the same weight (thickness) and width; there will be six horizontals woven into this pattern. Once you have the eleven folded over, add another horizontal spoke to prevent further slipping and movement.

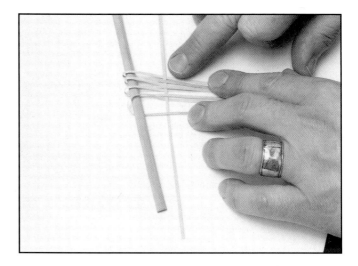

'Tighten the uprights and center them on the half-round stick. Once the third horizontal is in place the piece should be fully stabilized. Even up your weaving and finish adding the remaining horizontals. Use a flattened awl to straighten the horizontal spokes and to tighten the weaving much like a loom weaver does. Remember that the final spacing in the lid should be even and precise.

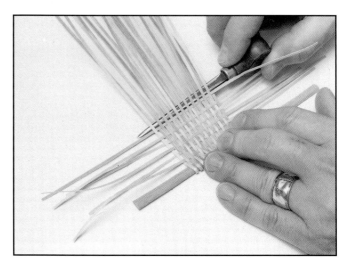

Select a thin weaver fairly close to the width of the uprights and horizontals that are already woven. Start to the right side and leave a length of the weaver duplicating the verticals and weave it into this pattern. This long end will in fact become the uneven rib enabling you to spiral the twill pattern. Fold over the weaver once you reach the half-round stick and weave down the pattern. You will be reversing the surfaces as you weave and the need for matching surface appearances will now be apparent.

In the photograph, the weaver has been woven in and is ready to turn the corner and begin twilling. Start the twilling with under two, over two, under two, over two, under two until you reach the center. The center of the first row is over three. Then back to under two, over two, etc. and come up the other side. Fold the weaver over the stick and start back the other way. The reversing back and forth will produce the semi-circular lid with the twill.

In the photograph, the center upright has been darkened for clarity and the weaver has overcast the left end of the stick and reversed. It is important to check your corners at this point to see that they are nice and neat. Because the weaver is turning at a right angle, it will eventually produce a little bump in the weaving — this is part of the look of the basket lid. If it is not to your liking, flatten it out by placing a book on top of it.

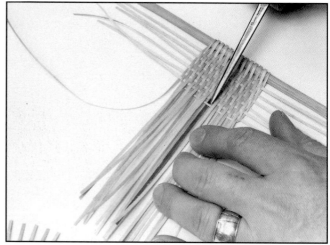

The next weaving pattern will be over one, under two, over two, under two, over two, under two until you get to the center. At the center point, you will be going over one. Repeat the pattern out from center. In the photograph you can see that the starting weaver has now become an upright. Remember that the weaving on the side is going to be equal to the weaving on the front edge or round edge. Keep it tight and neat. Use the flat awl or a stick to tighten and neaten the weaving.

third of four elements to this twilling design. This photograph shows the center pattern as it is emerging.

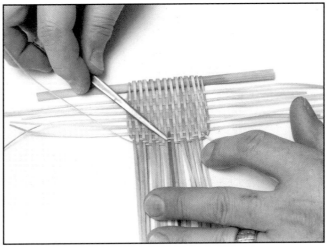

Begin to spread the uprights a little so that the weaving is tight. Take your time and make sure that the weaving does not twist.

The next pass is under one, over one, under two, over two, under two, over two, under three. Then repeat to the end and weave up the side as before. This is the

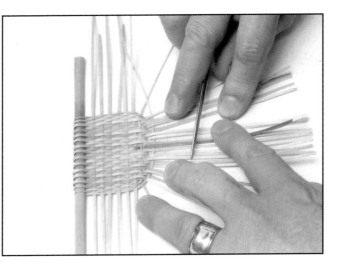

This photo shows how you would join a new piece of splint to continue weaving: end over the top of a rib and count back four; secure the new end underneath a rib and weave over the top of the lower weaver and continue to weave. You will have doubled weavers for a distance of four ribs. To prevent unsightly joins you can thin the overlapped weavers. Be careful not to join at the corners where there is stress.

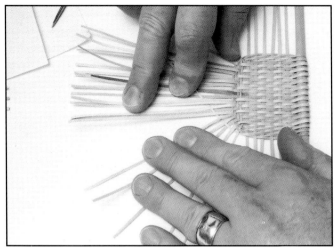

The last pass and final element of the design is over one, under one, over one, under two, over two, under two, over two, and at the center it changes to under one. Continue the pattern, then turn back and repeat the entire process. Spread the up-rights so that you get in closer and tighter. This spreading should make your angle turns at the "corners" neater. A continued spreading or fanning out of the uprights will even the distances between them and allow for a neat and even lashing.

In this view the diagonal pattern is finished. You may repeat the above steps as many times as you wish to widen out the lid. However, you have to decide on the next row (which is a repeat of step one) if that is where you want to stop the twilling. If that is the case, then you should finish up the patterns as required in the twill. The rest of the weaving will revert to simple over and under. In the photographs, the twilling pattern has been repeated, to create

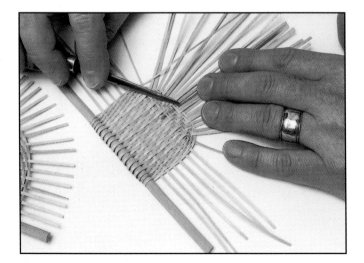

interest before stopping the pattern. Remember that if you repeat step one in the twilling pattern, you are beginning another twill sequence.

Once you have completed the final pattern sequence the weaving will be totally reverted to simple over and under. To widen the lid and lengthen it proportionally, you can now weave this simple pattern for as long as necessary.

To end the weaving, double back the weaver on itself, adjusting the weaving to allow this to happen, and cut it off underneath a rib to secure.

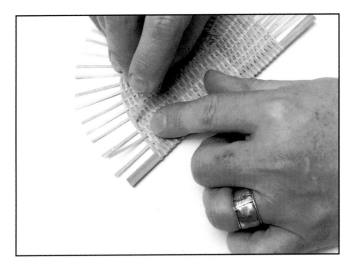

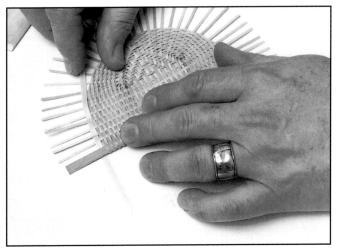

Start to weave in a wide band which is equivalent to the upright weight and about the width of the lasher that will wrap the rim. It should be long enough to go around the piece once and have sufficient length to secure the ends. Clip them carefully. Now the lid is ready for the lashing.

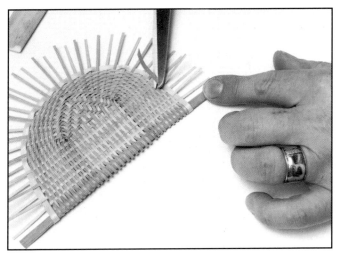

Use a cleaned lasher that is thinned slightly so as not to distort the rim. The length of the lasher should be a minimum of seven times the distance you will cover. It is better to have too much than too little. Secure the end and begin to lash on the diagonal between the spaces created by the ribs. Snug down the loops created by the lasher and fold them neatly as you continue. Be careful not to distort the rim. Secure the far end of the lashing as you began it.

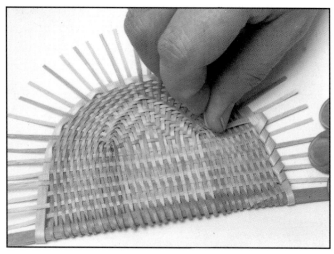

Now fold over the rib ends and secure them on a diagonal as you pass them through a loop created in the lashing process. Clip off the excess ends of the ribs after they have dried thoroughly. Shorten the stick to the desired length.

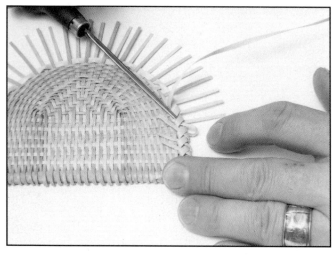

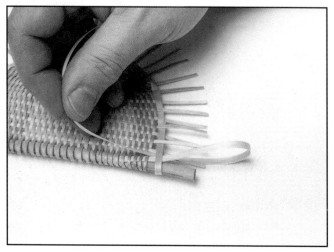

Drill the stick with two small holes and secure the lid with fine wire onto your basket. In the photograph, the fine wire hinges are shown securing the lids.

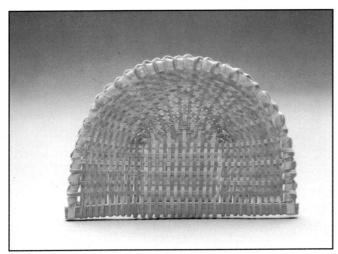

This is the pattern the Shakers chose to show to the outside. I prefer to show the braided edge. You decide which you prefer.

The photograph shows how I choose to secure the piece of wood that holds the lids in place between the handle. Drill through the handle and into the end of the stick, and then drive two carved pegs in place.

Antique baskets and their uses.

The functions and varieties of baskets are almost endless — wire and splint constructed baskets which served as colanders, utility or storage baskets, ox muzzles, cheese baskets, wood chip baskets, finely woven Ministry baskets, egg baskets, herb baskets, and a variety of smalls. This chapter includes selections from the Hancock Shaker Village Museum basket collection; many reflect the eclectic styles and makers characteristic of a working village. I have also included outstanding examples of Shaker baskets in private collections, as well as fine Native American and German baskets which were sold by the Shakers; these supplemental baskets augmented the dwindling Shaker output.

For nearly a hundred years the Shaker

basket industry has remained virtually extinct, yet Shaker baskets continue to climb in value and gain appreciation. These understated forms represent some of the finest basket artistry that this country has ever produced. The protected environment and spiritual nature of the Shakers' work surely contributed to this now publicized artistry.

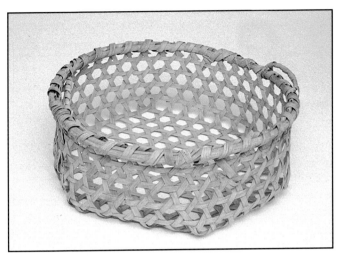

Cheese basket

Shaker strawberry baskets

Ox muzzle to prevent grazing

Manufactured utility basket

Below left - The Shakers often made baskets with a variety of inner compartments, used for sewing items and other small objects. Finer construction typified those of Shaker origin. This basket, however, is of Native American origin and shows a similar fineness.

Bottom left - Willow baskets such as this one were purchased and made by the Shakers and used in their daily activities. It is a mistake to attribute these baskets solely to origins other than Shaker. The Shakers used willow in their basketry, but the fine skein picnic baskets and some similiar items are of questionable Shaker origin.

Top right - Unusual four-handled splint basket, from Canterbury, N.H. The very high center helps spread out its contents and prevent the weight from centering in the bottom. Two sets of handles for a possible second person indicate that wet or heavy contents from the field were carried.

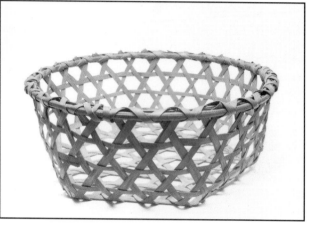

Middle right - Splint cheese (curd) baskets were often made by the Shakers and sold at handsome prices. Even large baskets used little material, yet prices could reach one dollar, high for the early 19th century. Lined with cheesecloth, such baskets allowed the whey to be drained from curds of cheese.

Bottom right - Wire basket with sturdy wire wrapped rims and oak weavers, often made at the shore and used to gather and rinse shell fish or root vegetables.

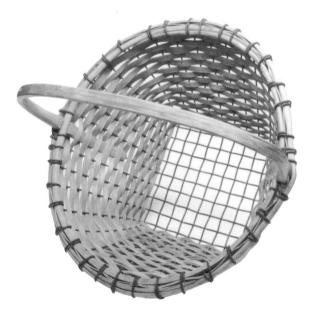

Top left - Splint lidded hexagon basket. This handled version, probably from Mount Lebanon, combines beauty and utility, a hallmark of the Shakers. Uses varied widely, and less refined versions even found their way into hen houses to collect eggs.

Bottom left - Fancy twilled double lidded basket, typical of the fine fancy work of the Shakers, often advertised in "broadsides" of the period. The word fancy referred to high quality often synonomous with the Shakers. Decorative design elements were never the focus, but were incorporated if also serving the function.

Top right - Sturdy baskets like this were used for many functions. The nail in the rim, securing the handle, dates this as a "recent" basket. The use of nails is not uncommon; the Shakers and others sometimes used them. While probably not of Shaker origin, such baskets easily found their way into Shaker workplaces as part of their commerce with the world's people.

Middle right - The use of ribbons and other features indicate turn of the century origin. Dwindling production was supplemented by Native American baskets meeting the high Shaker standards. Collectors should note that the small amount of swabbed color on this basket and the hinging indicate origins other than Shaker. Its functions are variable.

Bottom right - Leather-lined Shaker chip basket, probably from Canterbury, N.H. Leather protected the basket from wood chips, used to start fires in woodstoves.

Small fine skein willow basket, likely of German origin, could be used for holding fine handwork.

Multi-purpose Shaker open baskets, differences in appearance created in bottom pattern.

Bulbous work basket, possibly from Maine

Leather-lined work basket

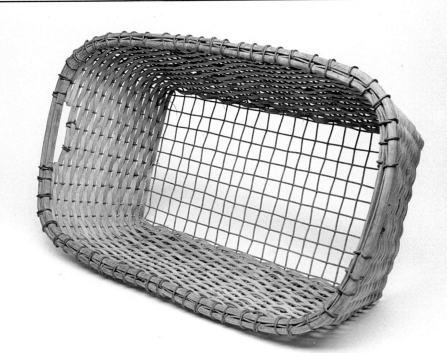

*Finely crafted
Shaker sister's bonnet*

Unusual wire basket with reed weavers, open handles
and sturdy wire-wrapped rim.

Open tray
of black ash

Contrasts and comparisons.

There is a great deal of confusion about the identification of Shaker baskets and frequently baskets by other peoples are mistaken for Shaker products. It is often a matter of subjectivity when a person attributes a basket to the Shaker communities, unless a clear attribution is possible — a match to an existing Shaker mould is the safest and clearest way to identify a Shaker basket. However, while extensively used by the Shakers, moulds were also used by other basketmakers.

Because the Shakers sold baskets other than their own, to supplement community income, identification is even more confusing. Antique dealers and other sellers frequently identify baskets as Shaker, based on a fineness of construction. They forget that other groups of makers showed spectacular sophistication in the construction of their work and this is simply not enough to call a basket Shaker. Materials used do not limit the spectrum of baskets made by the Shakers either. White oak, willow, black ash, poplar, swamp maple, and commercially available reed were frequently used in aspects of production.

Perhaps no group gets credit for making Shaker baskets more than the generations of basketmakers residing in Columbia County, New York. These baskets are nicknamed "bushwhacker" and Taghkanic. While beautifully constructed and enjoying rapidly increasing prices due to recent notoriety, they are not Shaker. Look at the handle treatment of the Taghkanic swing handle — the distinctive difference is how the handle is hinged to the rim and how the handle itself is constructed. The "ear" or "steeple" that allows the handle to pivot is more readily carved and is inserted to the inside and outside of the basket. The rims lock these simple notched ears in place. Other styles of ears in this type of basket are either inserted inside or outside of the basket, not straddling the basket. The other most obvious difference is that a hole is drilled in the ends of the handle, allowing it to swing. Native Americans frequently burned in such holes. The far more complicated swing handle of a basket in the Hancock Museum collection is the usual New England/Shaker style. Variations on this look are frequent, but this contrasting style is quite unique.

A number of "bushwhacker" baskets are included here to educate your eye about the look that characterized Taghkanic work. Notice that the rims appear to be more pronounced and when lashed to the basket seem oval in appearance. While not abrupt, they are far less integrated than in Shaker baskets; these baskets seem to be an assembly of parts rather than a more integrated flow of the shapes found in Shaker work.

Another difference is the carving and splint preparation. More carving is apparent and the splints show subtle, but slightly more hand-prepared effort. The weaving is spiraled upward with thin weavers and the weaving pattern makes use of a characteristic splint upright. The "end" handles on larger baskets appear slightly heavier and less exacting, and the shoulder or lug area above the rim sometimes seems high. Simple handled baskets have a "blocky" or thick edge (lug) on which the rim rests and the tab inserted into the basket is fairly short. The overall appearance of these "bushwhacker" baskets is fine enough to fool the "experts," but when individually analyzed the parts begin to tell the true story.

The way the rims are lashed also is somewhat different. The "bushwhacker" styles frequently show little care to concealing beginnings or ends, and the lashing is heavy and pronounced. The Shakers, however, were obsessive about concealing nearly all "detracting" details, especially on those baskets they sold. The Shakers varied the lashing styles on their baskets, whereas Taghkanic baskets appear exclusively cross bound.

While the Taghkanic made their share of smalls, the Shakers made thousands and sold them as fancy work. These Shaker smalls were finer in almost every respect. The size of the "bushwhacker" smalls were little but seemed over-scaled in materials, when contrasted with the Shaker production.

Miniature baskets of fine origins and hexagonally plaited styles are not only the work of Shakers as often thought. These miniatures were constructed by Germans and the Shakers purchased them for resale. The use of quaking aspen (poplar) as splints adds to the confusion, because these fine wood splints resemble the ash or poplar used by the Shakers.

Native American baskets are somewhat easier to distinguish because splint widths were frequently varied within a basket to produce a design element. Swabbed color and design elements are hallmarks as well. I have seen classic Shaker shapes produced by Native Americans that have colors swabbed on the weavers. Splints folded to the outside are also common, although not exclusive to Native American baskets. Extra strength was gained by this technique and the Shakers sometimes used it on larger baskets. Included here is a selection of Native American work and baskets of other origins to illustrate some styles that are often confused with Shaker, to help you be more informed about what is and what is not Shaker.

Nesting Taghkanic baskets,
showing characteristic ear insertion

Taghkanic, showing end handles, lugs

Taghkanic, showing rim
and spiral weave

Taghkanic, showing swing handle

Native American

Native America

with block stamped decoratio

Taghkanic tray and Native American smalls

Fine skein German willow baskets (left and center) and Native American splint basket (right). The Shakers made identical forms and are easily confused.

Glossary.

Algonkin/Algonquin - the people who speak Algonkian (or Algonquian) dialects, such as Mohegan, Narraganset, Ojibwa, Abnaki, Arapaho, and other tribes.

blasphemy - irreverence toward anything considered sacred.

boss - a circular protruberance or raised area used as ornamentation; used in handle description.

brother - male Shaker member of no special rank.

celibate - unmarried, especially by reason of religious vows.

chamfer - to bevel; the surface formed when cutting away the corner of two faces or surfaces of wood; referring to handles and rim detail.

chase weaving - a process of weaving with two weavers so an even number of uprights may be used.

circumference - the outside dimension of a circle; perimeter.

cleat - skid; extra addition to the underside of a basket that prevents direct wear.

cross bound - refers to alternating lashing or binding, in which the lasher strip is crossed over on the top of the rim, producing an X at the intersection.

dividing - to split into parts; in this book, refers to equal divisions (halving).

dividing box - used for splitting strips of ash into progressively thinner strips.

double up - to go over the top of lower material.

drawknife - exposed blade with two handles, used for shaving wood.

dressing - cleaning of the splints.

false rim - band of wider splint woven into the top of a basket, creating a rim-like appearance, and to which the actual rims are lashed.

family - Shaker unit of 30 - 100 members.

fancy - refers to high quality, grade "A".

felling - cutting down a tree.

finishing details - in this book refers to aspects of a basket that perfect, complete or are desirable.

fissured - cleaved or split, in reference to bark pattern.

flex - to bend or stress.

foot - runner, skid, or cleat, attached to a basket as a "wear barrier."

gouge - to scoop out a cavity or area.

growth cycle - can refer to one year of tree growth or collectively to life span.

handle - the means by which a basket is carried; various names were given to styles and some makers added their own personal carving expressions.

heartwood - the center part of the tree trunk; heartwood is darker than the outer sapwood.

hone - a fine whetstone for sharpening tools; to sharpen, dress.

increment borer - cutting device turned into a log, giving a small tubular cross section of the growth rings.

join - to splice or overlap two ends during weaving; area of attachment.

keeper - fine strip woven into bottom of basket to "lock" uprights in place before weaving.

lacing - sometimes used synonymously with lashing and binding.

lance-shaped - like a spear.

lasher - wide band of splint used to overcast or wrap the rim, holding the basket together.

lug - synonymous with shoulder; projects like an ear.

Millennial Law - Shaker rules and regulations set forth dealing with the operations of spiritual and temporal matters.

mould - mold, drum, form, block; wooden shape over which a basket is woven.

notched handle - a handle in which a groove or channel is cut to receive the rim.

order - Shaker level of membership.

overcast - slanted stitch-like lacing.

peat bog - wet spongy ground.

plaiting - simple over-under weaving.

puzzle - a basket mould that comes apart to allow easy removal of basket.

quarter - to divide into fourths, as in splitting out wood.

reed - a frequently used splint substitute that originates from the center "pithy" section of a climbing palm (rattan).

reference mark - mark used to line up pieces of a basket.

ribs - vertical members of a basket; also called uprights or spokes.

rim - half round or flattened strip with rounded corners that secures handle and strengthens the basket top; bent while flexible, it helps define shape of the basket.

runner - skate-like addition to the bottom of a basket that prevents wear and can be used as a winter skate for pulling the basket.

sapwood - outermost, light-colored porous wood that extends to the heartwood.

sawhorse - narrow beam supported by end legs; rack on which wood is laid to ease sawing.

sawtooth - having teeth like a saw; serrated edge.

scarf - to chamfer, halve, or cut away two pieces to correspond to each other.

score - line or long mark; scratch or incision.

shoulder - ridge or thickness in the handle placed to prevent disengaging from the basket.

sister - female Shaker member of no special rank.

sizing - cutting to a specific uniform size.

skate - runner or cleat added to basket bottom, allowing basket to be pulled on ice.

splint - in this book, refers to black ash pounded or divided along the tree's growth rings (not the same as commercially prepared splint).

splits - common reference to splints prepared by splitting out growth rings.

split out - to divide wood along growth rings with wedges, axe, hatchet, froe, or other splitting devices.

spiral - upward winding or circling, like the thread of a screw.

spokes - vertical members of a basket; also called uprights or ribs.

spokeshave - small traverse plane; adjustable blade often used for rounding.

subdivide - to make additional divisions beyond half.

swabbed - color that is wiped on, as in baskets swabbed with color.

tab - tip or end that "flaps" up.

taper - to narrow or make gradually thinner toward one end.

template - pattern used as a guide to form work.

thickness sander - a sander which allows for specific thickness to be set and attained.

triphammer - mechanical pounding device often used by blacksmiths; power hammer.

Trustee - Shaker man or woman who supervised business and legal affairs of a family with respect to the outside world; sometimes called office deacon or office sister. Trustees were Deacons or Deaconesses but not necessarily the reverse.

twilling - a pattern created by weaving over and under pairs of threads or ribs, in a particular sequence.

uprights - vertical members of a basket; also called standups, staves, spokes, or ribs.

weavers - horizontal strips interwoven with uprights to create the body of the basket.

whetstone - a stone for sharpening tools.

A Note About Suppliers.

Usually, the supplies you need for making the projects in Lark books can be found at your local craft supply store, discount mart, home improvement center, or retail shop relevant to the topic of the book. Occasionally, however, you may need to buy materials or tools from specialty suppliers. In order to provide you with the most up-to-date information, we have created a listing of suppliers on our Website, which we update on a regular basis. Visit us at www.larkbooks.com, click on "Craft Supply Sources," and then click on the relevant topic. You will find numerous companies listed with their web address and/or mailing address and phone number.

Black Ash

Hickory

White Ash

Index.

Miscellaneous photo credits.

Photos courtesy of Darrow School History Dept., New Lebanon, NY: pages 2 & 3, 6, 11, 18, 19, 20, 26, 30; Hancock Shaker Village: pages 25, 27, 31; Brian Lewis: page 21; Michael Schwartz collection, photo by Ellin Ente: page 138 (top right); Author's collection: pages 14, 15, 17, 37, 38 (top right).